THE STUDENT GRUB GUIDE

Alastair Williams

SUMMERSDALE

1st edition printed in 1991
Reprinted 1992 and 1993
2nd edition printed in 1995
Reprinted 1996
Copyright © by Summersdale Publishers 1995.

Available from

Summersdale Publishers
46 West Street
Chichester
West Sussex
PO19 1RP
United Kingdom

A CIP catalogue record for this book is available from the British Library.

ISBN 1 873475 24 1

Printed and bound in Great Britain
by Selwood Printing Ltd.

Cover design by Chloe Sitwell

Illustrations by Amanda Byfield

> **If you are thinking of writing a non fiction book, please contact the Editor at the above address.**

To my parents
with love and thanks

Alastair Williams was a student at numerous establishments of higher education before eventually graduating from Southampton. He has travelled throughout the world in his quest for mouth watering recipes that can easily be reproduced by any student, and this book is the result. Look out for his next book, *Man About The Kitchen*, due out soon!

Acknowledgments

I would like to thank the following people for the help they have given me with this book.

Stewart for helping throughout the year with editing and contributions and the odd cup of tea, without which this book would not have been possible. (Shame he can't cook though).

I would also like to say a big thank you to Chloe for her wonderful cover design and Mandy for the terrific illustrations.

Thanks to Maggie for her support and encouragement, and also to John Sanders for believing in me.

I must also thank my Mother, Grandmother, Peter, Clare, Julie, Barbara, Chris and Mike for their help.

Contents

Introduction

What's all this cooking stuff about?

Starting college

Higher education is supposed to do more than improve a person academically: the hope is that time spent at college will give students an opportunity to experience a wide range of activities and to mature as an adult...well, that's the theory anyway. Judge for yourself.

But starting college in new surroundings with new people can be daunting, and for those leaving the comfort and security of their home for the first time it may take some getting used to.

On the other hand there are those who can't wait to leave home, to escape from parents who always complain about loud music or untidy bedrooms. Arrival at college means that you have the freedom to do what you want, within certain physical and legal parameters.

Unfortunately, leaving home has its disadvantages. For example, you'll soon miss certain things: home cooking, someone to do the washing, someone to tidy up after you, and a parent's car with a full tank of petrol. Whether you are sharing a house, living in a self catering flat, or even in halls of residence, you'll have to learn to cope for yourself. This means cooking.

Food may well be a problem, and mistakes will be made in trying to solve it. Many students initially opt to live on takeaways, but there is a limit to how many chicken vindaloos your stomach can take, and precious grants can soon dwindle.

Aims of the book

It may seem that all is lost, but there is an alternative - pick up this book and get cooking. The object of this book is to give students a selection of recipes and advice that will enable them to get beyond the realms of cheese on toast or shrivelled jacket potatoes and to discover simple but tasty dishes. (Those who have yet to reach the realms of cheese on toast will nevertheless find ample recipes to get them going). The majority of the recipes in this book are designed to be cheap and easy to prepare, but there is also a section on more adventurous meals and advice on entertaining.

The emphasis of the book is on preparing and cooking main courses, but starters are included for those wanting to impress. And, of course, the all-important sections on desserts and cakes, snacks, breakfasts and booze cover most eventualities.

What you need

The chances are that your kitchen, as well as being a health liability, will lack the modern appliances that most family kitchens have. The idea of attempting a meal without a Magimix and its 101 attachments may seem daunting, but it can be done. From personal experience I know that most student kitchens will not even have set of scales, so many of the measurements given use spoons, and where ounces and grammes are used the amounts can often be converted using the chart that turns imperial and metric into more usable table and tea spoons.

You may also need patience. Many of the recipes given are quick and simple, but when attempting something more adventurous it is essential not to give up. There are going to be times when your souffle looks more like a pancake, but even the best chefs have the occasional disaster. Try to think of it as an act of God!

Some people will find cooking very easy, but they're probably swots anyway. The rest of us mere mortals need a little more perseverance and patience. But cooking disasters are all part of the fun, and experimenting with this book could lead to all sorts of wonderful experiences, some of which may even be of a culinary nature.

The basics

If you have had no experience of cooking, and judging from some of my friends who lived for three years on baked beans and toast, without the wit even to combine the two, this is likely, then you will need some help. Unfortunately, most cookery books tend to be marketed towards those who have experience in cooking, and they contain far too many irrelevant, expensive, impractical and unpalatable recipes for students. What would your housemates think if you were to serve them with a platter of marinated pigs' trotters? Rest assured, there are no monkey brains or goats' testicles to be found in this book.

Common sense

The recipes in this book are designed with simplicity in mind, both in terms of implements required and cooking skills. All that is needed is common sense - I don't want to be held responsible for a student who ends up in the hospital burns department for having misunderstood the instruction "stand in boiling water for 20 minutes".

Another important point to remember is that all cooking times and heats are approximate. Cooking is an instinctive thing and no amount of instructions can replace common sense and initiative.

There are a wide variety of recipes in this book. They range from cheap to expensive, from easy to prepare to being moderately difficult. The emphasis is on simple but interesting meals.

Before you try any recipe read through it first to make sure you have the ingredients and the time to prepare it.

While it is unusual for a person to have no cooking experience, here are some basic reminders, hints and guidelines for the beginner. Refer back to these basics when cooking full recipes.

How to cook rice

There are various types of rice available, but if you are trying to save your grant then buy the cheapest. Allow about 2 to 3 oz (50 to 75g) per person. If you don't have any scales, a mug holds about 8 oz (200g), so use that as a guideline.

Before cooking rice it is advisable to put it in a sieve and wash it. This removes some of the starch and will help to prevent it from sticking. After washing the rice, place it in a saucepan with a covering of water and cook according to the instructions on the packet. The time it takes depends on the type of rice used. The best way of testing it is to taste it...if it is still hard in the middle it needs a bit longer. Make sure that there is enough water in the saucepan, otherwise it will burn on the bottom.

Pasta

Allow roughly 2oz (50g) of pasta per person. See Italian section on cooking of pasta.

How to cook potatoes

Chips, crisps, mash - need I say more about the versatility this deceptively plain-looking discovery of Sir Walter? Yes, perhaps a little more needs to be explained...

There are two basic types of potato: new and old. Both are now available all year round, although new potatoes tend to be cheaper in the summer. Allow 1 or 2 potatoes per person, depending on your appetite and the size of the potato.

All potatoes need to peeled or scrubbed before cooking, unless you are preparing jacket potatoes.

There are many different ways in which you can cook potatoes. The most common way is to boil them. After peeling or scrubbing the potato, cut into halves or quarters, depending on its size, then place in salted boiling water for 15 to 20 minutes or until they are tender all the way through. If you want mashed potato make sure they are well cooked otherwise they will be lumpy. Drain the potatoes, add a nob of butter and a drop of milk, then using a potato masher squash until they are nice and creamy, adding more milk and black pepper if required.

Roast potatoes

Peel the potatoes, then halve or quarter them depending on their size. Parboil for 5 minutes in salted boiling water, then drain. Place the semi-cooked potatoes in a baking tray with some oil or lard and stick in the oven on Gas Mark 6 (425 Deg F, 220 Deg C) near the top of the oven if possible. Baste the potatoes with the oil a couple times while they are cooking. Roast the potatoes until they are golden and verging on crispiness, this should take between 60 and 90 minutes.

Chips

These things are almost a British institution, and they should of course be served with fish and wrapped in an old newspaper with lashings of vinegar and salt. If that description hasn't quelled your craving for chips then here is how to make your own.

Peel some old potatoes and cut into chip shapes. If you are feeling sophisticated slice them thinner into French fries. The next stage is potentially dangerous so take care. The chips need to be covered or at least partially covered in oil to cook, so a large amount of oil is needed.

Heat the oil in a large frying pan, then carefully add the chips, taking care not to throw them in the pan, otherwise hot oil will be splashed.

Fry the chips until they are crisp, making sure that the oil does not get too hot.

Whatever you do remember to turn the heat off. If your fat does catch fire it is imperative that you do the right thing.

The right thing

- Never throw water on top of the oil - this will make it worse.
- Turn off the gas if you can safely do so, otherwise wait until the fire is has been extinguished.
- The most effective way to put out a fat fire is to get a dampened tea towel and place it over the top of the pan. Leave it there until all the flames are gone.

Hygiene

If you are in a large shared house, the kitchen may have to cope with as many as seven, eight or nine people. Sometimes the kitchen also serves as the communal room, especially if the lounge has been turned into another bedroom. It is quite easy when there are large numbers of people sharing a small kitchen for it to come to resemble something out of The Young Ones. The situation is usually worse if it is a male-only house. Having been a student for a number of years I have had the opportunity to visit many student kitchens, and most of them were truly revolting - the washing up is normally only done when there are no more spare plates or cutlery available, or when parents or landlords came to visit.

It is a good idea if you are in a shared house to organise some sort of rota for cooking and cleaning. If one or two people cook each night for everyone it avoids the hassle that would occur if everybody in the house waited to use the cooker for themselves. It also means that you will only be cooking perhaps once or twice a week.

When your kitchen gets to the stage where you are sharing it with the rats and cockroaches, it's time to start worrying. Food that is left lying around for long enough will go off and harmful bacteria will evolve. If the green furry parts in your kitchen make it look more like a biology experiment than a hygienic place suitable for food storage and preparation, it might be a good idea to clear the whole kitchen and to disinfect it.

Apart from having clean kitchen surfaces, it is essential that the fridge is looked after too. If something is spilt make sure it is mopped up, and not left to fester.

It is important when buying meat that it is eaten within the recommended time on the packaging. If there is no label ask the supermarket assistant or butcher. The above applies not only to meat but to all products that have a limited life, like eggs, yoghurt etc.

Conversion chart

The recipes in this book are given in Imperial and Metric measurements, which are self explanatory, but many small amounts are measured in terms of spoons or cups.

The following abbreviations are used:

Tbs = Tablespoon (the one that's too big to put in your mouth)
Tsp = Teaspoon (what you put in your teacup)

Spoon measures can also be substituted for ounces with certain ingredients, which is handy for those without a set of kitchen scales. Obviously the weights of all ingredients will vary, but here are some rough measures...

1 Tbs= 1 oz (25g) of...syrup, jam, honey etc
2 Tbs= 1 oz (25g) of...butter, margarine, lard, sugar
3 Tbs= 1 oz (25g) of...cornflour, cocoa, custard powder, flour
4 Tbs= 1 oz (25g) of...grated cheese, porridge oats

All spoon measures refer to **level** spoons, not heaped.

1 mug of rice weighs roughly 8 oz (200g)

The approximations used for conversion between Metric and Imperial in this book are as follows . . .

1 oz	=	25g
1 lb	=	500g
1 fluid oz	=	25ml
1 pint	=	0.5 litre
1 inch	=	2.5 cm

In all recipes the oven should be heated to the temperature stated prior to cooking.

Glossary of cooking terms

Baste   To spoon fat or oil over food, to keep it moist. Usually done to a joint of meat whilst it is in the oven.

Beat   This is the mixing of ingredients using a wooden spoon, a fork or a whisk.

Chop   To cut into small pieces.

Cream   To mix fat with a another ingredient like sugar until it becomes creamy.

Dice   To cut into small cubes.

Grate   A grater can produce coarse or fine shavings of food, such as cheese or vegetables.

Knead   To use your knuckles to smooth dough out, the idea being to get a smooth texture.

Marinade   Can be a combination of juices, spices, or oils, in which meat is soaked to enhance the flavour.

Parboil   This is the partial boiling of something. The food will then normally be finished off by another method, eg roast potatoes.

Peel   To the remove the skin or the outer layer of a vegetable.

Rub in   To rub flour and fat together between your fingertips until they resemble breadcrumbs.

Simmer   To cook just below the boiling point, so that only an occasional bubble appears on the surface.

Healthy eating

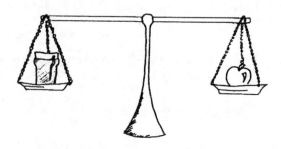

Healthy eating is something that many of us pay little thought to - youthful decadence is more fun, after all. But if your idea of a balanced diet means equal amounts of food to alcohol you should read this section.

Normally, when living at home and eating three square meals a day (presumably including plenty of vegetables and fruit), you will receive all the vitamins and minerals needed to stay healthy. All this can change when you go away to college. It is very easy to start skipping meals - most people I knew who lived in halls very rarely had breakfast, took only a sandwich or some chocolate for a quick, filling lunch, and then perhaps a baked potato with chips for dinner. This is not particularly healthy.

Those living in a shared house will find cooking easier than those living on their own: you can take turns to cook, and it is much easier and enjoyable cooking for a group than for just one. If you are living on your own try and find someone else to share meals with. Cooking for one is less efficient and less economical, and it can be hard to put in much effort. I sometimes can't be bothered to prepare vegetables when I'm alone.

Eating food does much more than fill your belly. It provides the energy for movement, allows the healing of wounds and instigates the production of protoplasm which helps to replace dead cells.

If you want to stay healthy you must have a balanced diet. There are certain things that are essential to obtaining this . . .

Carbohydrates

These are the provider of energy. They also happen to be the cheapest types of food and can be found in things like potatoes, bread and rice. Although these foods are always available in ample supply, take care to limit your own intake because an excess of carbohydrates leads to obesity.

Fats

These also provide energy for the body, but they take longer to digest than carbohydrates. This means they are useful for storing energy. Fat is present in dairy products like butter, margarine, milk, cheese and, of course, in meat.

Proteins

The word protein derives from the Greek word 'of first importance', and that is exactly what they are. Proteins are necessary for bodily development and repairs to damaged cells. Proteins are found in fish, lean meat, milk, cheese and eggs.

Vitamins

This is one area where many students fail to supply the correct amounts vital to keeping the body in perfect running order. The following is a list of the most essential vitamins and their sources . . .

Vitamin A

Vitamin A is present in dairy products like cheese, butter, milk and in green vegetables and liver.

Vitamin B

Vitamin B is made up of more than 10 different vitamins. They are to be found in whole grain cereals, liver, yeast, and lean meat.

Vitamin C

In the days of Nelson, scurvy was a common problem for a ship's crew. This is a disease resulting from a lack of vitamin C. The main source of the vitamin is citrus fruits like lemons, oranges, and blackcurrants and fresh vegetables. Ship owners discovered they could keep the scurvy at bay if the crew were given limes to suck during long periods at sea.

Vitamin D

A deficiency in calcium can lead to rickets in children, which means the bones are weak. In adults it can result in bow-legs. Vitamin D is found in milk, butter, cheese and liver.

Vitamin E

This is a vitamin that does not usually pose a deficiency problem in our society. It is found in milk, cheese, butter and meat.

Vitamin K

This is found in green vegetables. It helps the blood clotting process.

Roughage

This is vital if you want to keep all your passages open, or if you are having trouble making substantial deposits. High fibre cereals provide a good source of roughage.

Water

It may seem obvious that the body requires a substantial amount of water to function, but in case you forget this is a reminder.

Minerals

There are three main minerals whose continued supply can all too easily be jeopardised: iron, calcium and iodine. Other minerals such as the phosphates, potassium, magnesium and sodium are generally in good supply.

Iron

This is vital for the formation of the red blood cells. If a person has a deficiency of iron it can lead to anaemia. This is a shortage of red blood cells. Women find they are more prone to this than men, so it is important for them to have a high iron intake. Ensuring a high iron intake is not as simple as eating a bag of nails, however. Far better to eat liver, which is slightly more palatable, and is an excellent source of iron, as are other meats.

Calcium

This mineral is important for strong bones and teeth. It is found in dairy products like milk, butter and cheese.

Iodine

Iodine, although important, is not needed in the same quantities as calcium or iron. Fish is a good source of iodine.

Minerals and vitamins are available in pills from healthfood shops and supermarkets. Some contain multi vitamins, while others are more specific. It is still important to follow the recommended dosage.

The store cupboard

It is a common problem when cooking that whatever ingredients you have in your cupboard will always be the things you don't need, while whatever you do need will be conspicuous by its absence. You will also find that certain things in your cupboard will disappear almost immediately, like choccy biscuits, whilst Grandma's home-made chutney will stay lurking in the depths of the cupboard until you change house, or until the contents of the jar are used as a loose floortile adhesive.

Here is a suggested list of useful things to have in your cupboard:

Cans

Apart from the obligatory cans of lager, canned food is always useful for its longevity, and whole meals can often be prepared from one can.

Examples:

- Tomatoes *(used constantly throughout this book)*
- Sweetcorn
- Corned beef
- Tuna
- Anchovy
- Sardines
- Spaghetti
- Baked beans
- Ravioli
- Chick peas
- Kidney beans
- Soups
- Raspberries
- Strawberries
- Peaches
- Grapefruit segments
- Pineapple pieces/rings

Dry Goods

Cereals:	• Weetabix
	• Cornflakes
	• Shreddies
	• Bran flakes
	• Porridge oats
Flour:	• Self-raising
	• Plain
Pasta:	• Spaghetti
	• Tagliatelli
	• Shells
	• Tortolinni
	• Quills
	• Penne etc
Dried Fruits:	• Sultanas
	• Currants
	• Raisins
	• Glace cherries
Nuts:	• Almonds
	• Peanuts
	• Walnuts
Rice:	• Long grain
	• Basmati
	• Patna
Sugars:	• Caster
	• Granulated or golden granulated
	• Brown
	• Icing
Coconut:	• Dessicated
	• Soluble
Packet sauces:	• Bread
	• Cheese
	• Parsley

Cornflour

Custard powder

Baking powder

Biscuits

Vegetables

It's all too easy to leave out vegetables from a low budget diet: students often fail to balance their diet in this respect. The only vegetable with which they are familiar is usually the 'couch potato'.

Prepared to mend your ways? Rather than sticking with humdrum peas and carrots, try experimenting with the more exotic vegetables that are available in supermarkets these days.

Below is a list of some of the common and not-so-common vegetables currently available, explaining how they should be prepared and various ways of cooking them.

Aubergine Cut the top and bottom off and then slice thinly. Sprinkle lightly with salt and leave for 10 minutes. Before cooking, rinse the slices in water. The usual method for cooking aubergines is to fry them either in oil or butter until they soften.

Baby sweetcorn These are an expensive import from the Orient, but as with mangetout they are worth the price. The only preparation needed is washing, following which they can be gently boiled or fried. To benefit from their full flavour they need to retain their crispness.

Beans - French Wash them and top and tail. Cut into 1 inch lengths, or leave whole. To cook place in boiling water with a little salt and cook for 10 to 15 minutes. After cooking they can be tossed in butter.

Broccoli Wash in cold water, cut off the stalks then divide into flowerets. That means breaking off into clumps. Cook in boiling water for about 10 minutes. It is important not to over-cook broccoli because it will go mushy and lose most of its flavour.

Brussel sprouts Remove the outer leaves and cut off the stalk. It should not be removed entirely, otherwise all the leaves will fall off. Cut a cross in to the base and then wash in cold water. Boil in water with a pinch of salt for 10 minutes.

Cabbage There are three main varieties of cabbage: green, white and red. Remove the rough outer leaves and the centre stalk. You can either shred the leaves or perhaps quarter them. To cook the shredded cabbage place in boiling water for about 5 minutes. If the leaves are bigger they will need about 10 minutes.

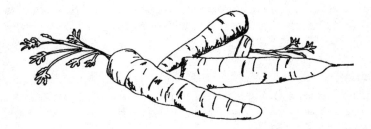

Carrots Top and tail the carrots and then either using a scraper or a knife remove the outer surface. Before cooking they can be quartered or sliced. Baby carrots can be cooked whole. Cook in boiling water for 15 to 20 minutes. Carrots can be eaten raw in salads etc. They also be roasted in oil when cooking a roast dinner.

Cauliflower Wash in cold water and then divide into flowerets. Cook in salted boiling water until tender - this should take about 10 minutes, depending on the size of the flowerets. Cauliflower can also be eaten raw and used for crudities at parties.

Courgettes Having been force fed these things for years I have almost come to like them. First of all give them a wash, then top and tail them. Slice thinly and fry in butter or oil for about 10 minutes.

Leeks Definitely a favourite with the Welsh. Remove the top dark green bit and the roots and wash. They can either be sliced into rings, quartered or even left whole. To cook either boil for 10 to 15 minutes or fry in oil or butter for about 10 minutes.

Mangetout If you haven't seen these before, they look like pea pods that have been squashed by a lorry. But they taste delicious and are almost worth the extortionate amount you will be charged for them.

To prepare your mangetout, wash and top and tail them. If boiling them, they need only 3 or 4 minutes because they maintain their flavour better when still crisp. They can also be fried gently in butter for a few minutes until they soften slightly. They make a colourful addition to stir fries.

Mushrooms If you are studying near the countryside you could try and find some wild mushrooms, but I don't mean those of the Paul Daniels variety (no recipes for space cakes in this book). Be careful not to pick any toadstools.

Anyway, once you have found or bought your mushrooms, wipe them with a clean damp cloth. Either remove or trim the stalk and then slice or leave whole. The mushrooms can be fried or grilled. To fry, melt a little oil or butter in a frying pan and cook for about 3 to 4 minutes, depending on size. To grill, put under a hot grill with a light covering of butter.

Onions The best way to stop your eyes watering when chopping onions is to get someone else to do it. Top and tail the onion first, then peel off the outer layer. It can be chopped or sliced into rings. Onions are normally fried in oil for about 5 minutes. They can be boiled in salted water for about 10 minutes.

Parsnips Top and tail, then peel and chop into largish pieces or thick slices. They can be boiled, fried or roasted.

To boil, place in boiling water with a pinch of salt for about 20 minutes or until they are tender.

If they are to be fried they need to be cut into thin slices or chips, otherwise they will not cook all the way through.

Perhaps the nicest way of cooking parsnips is to bake them. Place the parsnips in an ovenproof dish with a couple of tablespoons of oil and bake in a hot oven for about 40 minutes. They can be basted as if they were roast potatoes.

Peas If you have fresh peas, ie still in the pod, shell them and wash in cold water. To cook peas, place them in boiling water for about 10 minutes.

Peppers The most commonly available peppers available are the red and green ones, although there are yellow and orange varieties. They all have different flavours - the lighter in colour they are the sweeter they are, so the yellow ones are the sweetest and the green ones the most bitter.

Top and tail, then core and remove all the seeds. Slice into rings then halve and fry in a little oil for 5 minutes or so. They can also be eaten raw and are particularly nice in salads.

Potatoes See **Basics.**

Pumpkin If you have a whole pumpkin, cut into 4 then remove all the seeds and pulp from the inside. Remove the skin and cut into chunks. To boil, place in salted boiling water for about 30 minutes.

After the pumpkin has been boiled it can be fried in butter for 5 minutes.

Spinach The magic green weed that did wonders for Popeye hasn't yet had much effect on me! When buying spinach, buy more than you would if it was cabbage, for spinach will shrink considerably during cooking. Discard any yellowed leaves, then place in a small amount of boiling water for about 10 minutes. Grated nutmeg and spinach taste good together.

Swede Although this is not perhaps a vegetable you would normally choose to cook, it can provide an interesting alternative to 'chips and that'. Peel and chop into chunks, then wash in cold water. Cook in salted boiling water for 20 to 25 minutes or until tender. Can be mashed with a nob of butter and black pepper.

Sweetcorn Remove the husks and the ends, then place in boiling water for 10 minutes. Drain, then serve with butter and fresh black pepper.

Tomato Fresh tomatoes can be fried in butter or grilled. To remove the skin of a tomato, which should be done when making sauces, place in boiling water for about a minute. Remove from the hot water and cool them in cold water. The skins should now come away easily.

Turnip The limit of Baldrick's aspirations in life is the acquisition of what he calls his dream turnip. For those of similar ambitions, here is how to prepare your turnip: peel and cut into chunks, then place in boiling water for 20 to 25 minutes or until tender.

Spices, herbs, seasonings and flavourings

Given moderate use, these can transform a plain tasting meal into something special. Just remember the amounts used have to be carefully controlled, the idea being to enhance the flavour of the food, not to annihilate your taste buds.

When the recipes say salt and pepper it generally means a pinch of each, but it is up to the individual to season according to taste. One of the most essential items in a kitchen should be a pepper mill. Freshly ground pepper tastes so much better than the stuff that is pre-ground, so try and get hold of one.

Basil	Flavourings	Parsley
Bay Leaves	essences	Paprika pepper
Black pepper	Garlic	Rosemary
Capers	Garam masala	Sage
Caraway seeds	Ginger	Salt
Cayenne seeds	Lemon juice	Soy sauce
Chillies	Mace	Sweet and sour
Chilli powder	Marjoram	Tabasco
Chutney	Mint	Thyme
Chives	Mustard: French	Worcester
Cinnamon	English	Vinegar: cider
Cloves	Oregano	malt
Curry powder	Nutmeg	wine

Dressings and sauces

The use of the sauces and dressings can provide an exciting accompaniment to many otherwise plain tasting dishes.

Cheese sauce

This sauce is used in many of the recipes in this book, such as lasagne or cauliflower cheese.

Ingredients

1 pint (0.5 litre) of milk
4 oz (100g) of grated cheese
2 oz (50g) of margarine
2 oz (50g) of plain flour
Salt
Pepper

Melt the margarine in a small saucepan, but don't let it brown. Then stir in the flour and cook gently for a couple of minutes. The combination of margarine and flour is called a Roux, and it is also the name of the method of preparation.

Remove the Roux from the heat and add a little of the milk. It has to be added gradually otherwise it will end up being lumpy. Stir the milk in until a smooth consistency is achieved, then add the rest of the milk. When all the milk has been added return the pan to the heat, add the cheese and bring to the boil. Simmer for five minutes or so until the sauce has thickened.

Parsley sauce

This sauce is normally served with fish, but can be served with almost anything. The quantity can be halved if a smaller amount is needed.

Ingredients

1 pint (0.5 litre) of milk
2 oz (50g) of plain flour
2 oz (50g) of margarine
4 tbs of chopped fresh parsley
Salt
Pepper

The method for this sauce is as above, except the parsley is added just before serving.

French dressing

There are many variations of French dressing, and most people have there own favourite combinations. Olive oil is a must for an authentic tasting dressing, vegetable although much cheaper will not taste as good. Here are a few ideas...

It is unlikely that you are going to need vast quantities of the stuff so as a guideline use 4 parts olive oil to 1 part wine vinegar. A dash of French mustard, pepper, oregano or lemon juice can be added for more flavour. Place all the ingredients together in a small screw-top jar, and shake to combine the flavours.

Yoghurt dressing

Ingredients

1/4 pint (125ml) of plain yoghurt
1 tbs of lemon juice
Salt
Pepper

Mix the yoghurt and lemon juice together, season according to taste.

Soups and Starters

Also known, though not in student circles, as entrees and hors d'oeuvres. Guaranteed to shock your dinner guests into thinking that you have been somewhat frugal with the grub, so it is important to emphasise that this is only a starter, in order that they realise the extent of your sophistication.

These dishes are obviously intended for special occasions, and are not designed to fit in with the typical weekly budget. But the soup recipes can make a filling meal in themselves, and simply by increasing the portions some of the other recipes can be served as main dishes.

Garlic bread

This has to be another classic student recipe. It always goes down well at parties and is easy to make, though its resultant effect on the breath can limit one's amorous aspirations.

Ingredients

French stick
6 oz (150g) of butter
2 cloves of garlic
Tin foil

Put the butter in a small mixing bowl. Finely chop the garlic and add to the butter, blending it in with a fork. Slice the French stick at 2 inch intervals, without actually severing it, and spread some of the butter on both sides of each slit. Then close up the gaps and wrap the loaf in foil. Place in the oven and cook for 15 to 20 minutes at Gas Mark 5 (400 Deg F, 200 Deg C).

Mushrooms with garlic butter

Garlic again...well, you either love it or hate it. Personally I adore the stuff (is that why I'm still single?).

Ingredients

4 oz (100g) of mushrooms
4 oz (100g) of butter
2 cloves of garlic, peeled and finely chopped

Remove the stalk of the mushrooms then wash. Mix the butter and the garlic together with a fork and then spread on top of the mushrooms. Bake in the oven for 15 minutes on Gas Mark 5 (400 Deg F, 200 Deg C).

Mini sausages with honey and rosemary

This has to be one of my favourite dishes - just writing about it makes me drool! Fresh rosemary is a must, though.

Ingredients

Pack of mini sausages
Handful of fresh rosemary
3 tbs of runny honey

Arrange the sausages in a baking dish, prick with a fork, spoon on the honey, then place the rosemary on top. Bake in the oven on Gas Mark 6 (425 Deg F, 220 Deg C) for about 25 minutes, turning occasionally so they brown evenly.

Grilled grapefruit

This is a very quick and tasty way of serving grapefruit, and it does not have to be confined to a starter. It could be served as a snack for lunch or part of a late supper.

Serves 2

Ingredients

1 grapefruit
2 tsp of soft brown sugar
1 tsp of butter
1/2 tsp of cinnamon

Cut the grapefruit in half and remove the pips. Loosen the segments using a grapefruit knife. Put a teaspoon of brown sugar on each half with the butter and a light sprinkling of cinnamon. Place under a hot grill for five minutes.

Devils on horseback

This another one of those baffling, nondescript names that puzzles me.

Ingredients

Tin of prunes
5 rashers of streaky bacon
Cocktail sticks

Wash the prunes in cold water then remove the stones. Remove the rind from the bacon then cut each rasher in half. Wrap each prune in a piece of bacon then secure it by pushing a cocktail stick through the middle and place on a baking tray. Bake in the oven, until the bacon is slightly crisp, at Gas Mark 6 (425 Deg F, 220 Deg C)

Hummus

This one is a dip that can be served with freshly chopped vegetables (crudities) or pitta bread. Although Hummus is available in tins or even from your local delicatessen, it is cheaper to make your own. Having said that, I find it easier to use canned chick peas instead of soaking dried ones for hours. Note that a blender is needed for this recipe.

Ingredients

1 can of chick peas
2 cloves of garlic, peeled and finely chopped
Juice of 1 lemon
2 tbs of olive oil
4 oz (100g) of natural unsweetened yoghurt
1/2 tsp of ground cumin

Put all the ingredients in a blender and let them have it! Switch off when a soft consistency is achieved. Then put in a dish and chill for an hour or two.

Soups

Soups can be made as a lunchtime snack, as a starter, or in some cases as a light meal.

Tomato soup

Serves 4

Ingredients

1 lb (500g) of tomatoes
1 onion, peeled and finely chopped
Bouquet garni (little bag of herbs)
1 oz (25g) of flour

1 pint (0.5 litre) of water
1/2 pint (0.25 litre) of milk
1 tbs of oil
Salt and pepper

Boil some water in a saucepan, then place the tomatoes in it. Remove the pan from heat and leave for about 5 minutes. This is the best way of skinning a tomato. After this, remove the tomatoes from the water and peel off the skins. Chop into small pieces.

Fry the tomatoes and onions gently in the oil for about 15 minutes until they go mushy. Add the water and bouquet garni, then simmer for 1 hour. If you don't want bits in your soup, sieve the mixture. Otherwise, just add the flour and milk to the tomato mixture. Simmer for about 3 minutes, then serve.

French onion soup

Serves 4

Ingredients

2 large onions, peeled and thinly sliced
1 1/2 pints (0.75 litre) of vegetable stock
1 tbs of yeast extract
1 tbs oil
Black pepper
Salt
1 tsp of mixed herbs

Using a large saucepan, fry the onions in the oil for about 5 minutes. Then add the other ingredients and boil. After this, simmer for 15 to 20 minutes, and serve with grated cheese on top.

Vegetable soup

There are no limits as to what vegetables you can use. These are just a guideline. Serves 4.

Ingredients

2 tbs of oil
1 onion, peeled and chopped
1 leek, thinly sliced
2 cabbage leaves, shredded or finely chopped
1 courgette, finely chopped
1 carrot, scraped and sliced
1 bay leaf
2 pints (1 litre) of vegetable stock
Salt
Pepper

Heat the oil in a large saucepan, then fry the onions for about 5 minutes or until they have softened. Then add the other vegetables and fry for a further 10 minutes. Add the stock, season, bring to the boil, then simmer for 30 minutes. Remove the bay leaf before serving. If you want a smoother tasting soup then liquidise before serving.

Parsnip and apple soup

A liquidiser is required for this recipe.

Serves 4

Ingredients

2 tbs of oil
1 large onion, peeled and chopped
1 1/2 lb (750g) parsnips, peeled and chopped
1 apple, peeled and cored

2 pints (1 litre) of vegetable stock
Salt
Pepper

Heat the oil in a large saucepan, then fry the onions for about 5 minutes until they have softened. Add the apple and the parsnips and fry gently for a couple of minutes. Add the stock and bring to the boil, then simmer for 30 minutes. Transfer the soup into a liquidiser and blend until smooth. Serve with fresh crusty bread.

Types of meat

Vegetarians can skip this section, but those carnivores out there can now indulge in mental images of fillet steak and Sunday roasts. Students often find themselves unable to afford meat, other than fast-food burgers, on a regular basis, but I would advise against anyone resorting to microwaving next door's cat. Although the price of meat has risen lately (which won't affect those with access to a 12 bore shotgun and handy field full of bunnies), chicken is still relatively inexpensive, and certain cuts of red meats (and that doesn't just include the offal) shouldn't break the bank.

Beef

When choosing a piece of beef it should be a light red colour and slightly elastic, with not too much gristle. But if it contains no gristle it will have a poor flavour.

There are many different cuts of beef, and each is suitable for different methods of cooking:

Roasting
- Topside
- Sirloin
- Fillet
- Ribs
- Rump

Grilling or Frying
- Sirloin
- Fillet
- Rump
- Entrecote
- Minced

Stewing
- Rump
- Brisket
- Flank
- Chuck

Pork

Pork is cheaper than beef and should be a pale red colour.
It is important when cooking pork that it is sufficiently done
the danger in eating undercooked pork is that tapeworms
can take a fancy to your stomach. The meat should be white,
not pink, after cooking.

Roasting	· Ribs
	· Loin
	· Leg
	· Bladebone

Grilling or frying	· Chops
	· Ribs
	· Loin

Lamb

Lamb should be a pinkish red colour, and the bones at the
joints should be red.

Roasting	· Shoulder
	· Leg
	· Best end of neck
	· Loin

| **Grilling or Frying** | · Loin chops or cutlets |
| | · Liver |

Stewing	· Loin
	· Leg
	· Breast
	· Liver

Chicken

When buying chicken it should smell fresh and the flesh
should be firm. Chicken is very versatile: most parts can be
fried, roasted, stewed etc.

Main Dishes

This is the most important section of this book, because although there are sections on starters, making cakes etc, my experience as a student tells me there is little time to bake cakes, and the greatest efforts are made when cooking main meals for a whole household. The main meals in this book have an international flavour with the recipes being set out according to country of origin. Some of the recipes can lay claim to belonging to more than one country, so don't moan if you think something is in the wrong place.

The mixture of recipes is diverse, ranging from the standard student dishes like spag bol, chilli con carne, shepherd's pie etc to the lesser known and slightly exotic dishes. None are too complicated, though some are unusual. Don't be put off by the title of a particular recipe - read it through first, as names can be deceptive. And don't worry if your household lacks perhaps one or two of the minor ingredients, since it will probably not matter.

For those that think that any of the recipes are a bit on the expensive side, just remember that most of them could be prepared for the cost of a few pints of beer.

British

The traditional British fare is often thought of by foreigners as comprising of only bangers and mash, jellied eels and early morning fry-ups. This is absolutely true, and I can thoroughly recommend a pan full of greasy eggs, bacon and sausages after a hard night studying the local brews.

But things are changing fast, and mangetout could at this rate soon replace mushy peas on the school menus. I have to say, though, that petite portions of nouvelle cuisine are hardly sufficient to feed the average beer belly. With that in mind, I have endeavoured to preserve some vital remnants of our heritage in the following recipes:

Shepherd's Pie

This popular dish is supposed to use leftover beef from a Sunday roast, but minced beef is an adequate substitute for those not indulging in a roast. This recipe has many variations: I prefer to use the one that includes tomatoes, but try both and see which one you like.

Serves 3 to 4

Ingredients

1 lb (500g) of minced beef
1 onion, peeled and chopped
1 clove of garlic, peeled and finely chopped
1 tin of tomatoes (14 oz), optional
1 tbs of tomato puree
1 tsp of mixed herbs
Salt
Pepper
2 tbs of oil
5 medium potatoes, peeled

Heat the oil in a largish saucepan, add the onion and garlic, and fry for 3 to 4 minutes. Add the meat and cook for another 10 minutes, then add the other ingredients, and simmer for 15 minutes.

While this is simmering, cook the potatoes (test them with a knife - the knife should pass through the potato easily), then mash them with a nob of butter and a bit of milk. Put the meat in an ovenproof dish and cover with the potato, then put under the grill until the potato browns.

Bubble and squeak

This requires scraping the leftovers from the previous day/week out of the bin-liner, then melting it down to a substance slightly less chewy than industrial glue.

Ingredients

2 tbs of oil
Mashed potato
Greens or brussel sprouts
Egg
Whatever else has got stuck to it overnight

Fry the mixture until it smells edible, then eat if you dare.

Spicy sausage casserole

This is ideal for those fed up with boring old sausages and spuds. It is not a traditional English recipe, but I don't know where it originates from, so as I'm English it can stay here.

Serves 4

Ingredients

1 pack of pork sausages, cut into pieces (not the pack)
1 onion, peeled and chopped
2 cloves of garlic, peeled and finely chopped
1 tin of tomatoes (14 oz)
2 tbs of tomato puree
1 green pepper, seeded and chopped
1/2 pint (0.25 litre) of beef stock
2 tsp of chilli powder
Tsp of oregano
2 tbs of oil
Pepper
Salt

Heat the oil in a largish saucepan or wok, then fry the onions, garlic and chilli powder for about 5 minutes. Then add the sausages and the pepper, and cook for about 10 minutes. Add the tomato puree, beef stock, seasoning, tomatoes and oregano. Simmer for at least 15 minutes then serve with rice and peas. Alternatively after cooking the rice and peas add them directly to the casserole and cook for another couple of minutes.

Cauliflower cheese

A quick and cheap dish that even a Philosophy student can prepare with ease.

Serves 3 to 4

Ingredients

1 cauliflower
3/4 pint (350ml) of milk
1 oz (25g) of cornflour
Pepper
6 oz (150g) of cheese, grated

Prepare the cheese sauce as outlined in the chapter, Dressings and sauces, (using 4 oz/100g of the cheese) but use 3/4 pint (375ml) of milk instead of a pint (0.5 litre). Break the cauliflower into flowerets (clumps) then place in boiling water for about 10 minutes, making sure it is not overcooked.

When the cauliflower is cooked, drain well and place in an ovenproof dish, pour over the cheese sauce, sprinkle the other 2 oz (50g) of cheese and brown under a hot grill.

Toad in the hole

A classic dish that is about as misleading as hedgehog crisps.

Serves 4

Ingredients

1 lb (500g) of sausages
1 oz (25g) of lard
4 oz (100g) of flour
1 egg
1/2 pint (0.25 litre) of milk
A pinch of salt

Mix the flour and the salt, then make a well in the flour and break the egg into the well. Add first a little milk to give a smooth texture, then pour in the rest of the milk and beat for a minute or so. Put the sausages in a baking tin with the lard and bake for 10 minutes at Gas Mark 7 (450 Deg F, 230 Deg C). Then add the batter and cook for a further 25 minutes or until the batter has risen and is browned.

Beef stew

Serves 4

Ingredients

1 lb (500g) of stewing steak
1 onion, peeled and roughly chopped
1 clove of garlic, peeled and chopped
1 1/2 oz (40g) of flour
1 pint (0.5 litre) of beef stock
3 carrots, scraped and chopped
Bouquet garni
2 tbs of oil
Salt
Pepper

Put the oil in a casserole dish and fry the onions and garlic for 5 minutes. Cut the meat into 1 inch (2.5cm) pieces and roll them in the flour with a little salt and pepper. Fry for 5 minutes or until brown, and add to the onion. Add the rest of the flour to the pan and fry gently. Add the stock and boil until it thickens. Pour the sauce over the meat, add the bouquet garni and carrots, and bake at Gas Mark 4 (350 Deg F, 180 Deg C) for one to two hours.

Liver with bacon

Not everyone's favourite meal, but cheap and full of iron. Or is it lead?

Serves 4

Ingredients

2 tbs of oil
1 lb (500g) of liver (Medical students - this means lamb or pigs liver, not the leftovers from a dissection exercise)
1 large onion, peeled and chopped
3 rashers of whatever bacon you can lay your hands on
Flour for coating the liver
Pepper

After heating the oil in a frying pan, add the onion and fry for about 5 minutes. Add the bacon and liver to the onions, season, and cook for about 10 to 15 minutes.

Pork and cider casserole

This is a recipe that was achieved by experimentation, but the end result is most pleasing.

Serves 4

Ingredients

2 tbs oil
1 large onion, peeled and chopped
2 cloves of garlic, peeled and finely chopped
1 tin of tomatoes (14oz)
1 tbs of tomato puree
2 tsp of herbes du Provence
1 green pepper, cored and chopped
1 courgette, sliced
4 pork chops
1 pint (500ml) of dry cider
1 mug of macaroni
1/2 mug of frozen peas

Heat the oil in a large casserole dish, then fry the onion, garlic and green pepper for about 5 minutes. Then add the pork chops and fry on both sides for a couple of minutes. Add the tomatoes, puree, herbs, courgette, seasoning and cider then bring to the boil.

Simmer for about 40 minutes, adding the macaroni about 10 minutes before serving and the peas about 5 minutes before. Check to see if the macaroni is cooked before serving.

If the casserole begins to get a little dry add some water or more cider. Serve to the tune of *I Am The Cider Drinker* by *The Wurzels*.

Gammon steaks with pineapple

Serves 4

Ingredients

4 gammon steaks
Butter
4 pineapple rings

Salt
Pepper

Cook the gammon under a hot grill with a nob of butter for about 5 minutes each side. Season, then place a ring of pineapple on each and grill for another couple of minutes. Luvly served with mashed spuds and peas.

Chicken casserole

Serves 4

Ingredients

4 pieces of chicken (either breast, wings or thigh)
1/2 pint (0.25 litre) of chicken stock
1 tbs of tomato puree
1 onion, peeled and chopped
2 tsp of flour
Salt
Pepper
2 tsp of oregano or mixed herbs

Mix the flour with a little water and then add to the chicken stock. Add the herbs, onion, tomato puree, salt and pepper. Put the chicken in an ovenproof dish, and pour the stock over it. Cover the dish with foil and bake in the oven for 45 minutes. Serve with potatoes and vegetables.

Corned beef hash

This is one of my favourite cheapo meals. Corned beef suffered a slump in sales when they found companies had been using horse meat as a substitute. However that was many years ago, and it tastes OK to me.

Serves 4

Ingredients

2 tbs of oil
1 tin of corned beef
1 large onion, peeled and chopped
Milk
Butter
4 large potatoes
Salt
Pepper

Peel the potatoes and chop them into quarters. Place the potatoes in a saucepan of boiling water and boil for about 20 minutes or until tender. Then drain them and mash with a little milk and butter. Fry the onions in a large frying pan with the oil for about 5 minutes or until they are golden. Open the tin of beef and chop up into small pieces and add to the onion. Heat the beef through and then add the mashed potato. Fry until the potato turns slightly crispy, but not burnt. Best served with baked beans.

Minced beef and onions

Mince is still good value, and provides a good basis for many student meals. If you have never tried soya mince, it is not as bad as people make out, so why not give it a try and save yourself a few spondoolies?

Serves 4

Ingredients

2 tbs of oil
1 lb (500g) of minced beef
1 onion, peeled and chopped
1/2 pint (0.25 litre) of gravy
4 oz (100g) of frozen peas
Salt
Pepper

Pour the oil in a frying pan and fry the onions for about 5 minutes. Add the beef, season and cook for another 10 minutes. Mix up the gravy according to the instructions on the packet and add to the mince with the peas. Simmer for about 5 minutes and serve with potatoes.

If you want a bit more flavour try adding a few herbs or even a couple of teaspoons of chilli powder.

Courgette and bacon bake

Don't bother with this recipe if you can't stand courgettes.

Serves 4

Ingredients

2 tbs of oil
2 lb (1 kg) of courgettes, sliced
4 oz (100g) of bacon, cut into pieces
4 eggs
5 oz (125g) of grated cheddar cheese
3/4 pint (350ml) of milk
Salt
Pepper
1 oz (25g) of butter or margarine

Fry the courgettes for 4 to 5 minutes, then add the bacon and fry for another couple of minutes. Beat the eggs together with the milk, add the cheese and season. Grease a baking dish and layer the courgettes and bacon until they are used up. Pour the egg and cheese mixture over the courgettes, put the rest of the cheese on top, and bake at Gas mark 4 (350 Deg F, 180 Deg C) for 40 minutes or until golden.

Sausages

The great British banger is one of the country's most famous and highest renowned inventions. After all these years it still provides a cheap, simple and cholesterolly dangerous meal. Sausages come in various types, the most popular variants containing either pork or beef. The price will depend on their fat content - the cheapest might be almost pure tubes of fat. Handmade sausages can still be found at some local butcher shops.

Before cooking your sausages, get a fork and stab them a couple of times. This prevents splitting.

The usual methods for cooking sausages are frying or grilling. For those who want to minimise the relative unhealthiness of the sausage, grilling is the better way to choose.

To fry: heat some oil in a frying pan, and fry the sausages for 15 to 20 minutes. Turn them regularly when cooking to make sure they brown and cook evenly.

To grill: remember to prick the sausages, then grill for about 10 minutes on each side, on a medium heat.

Serve with finger rolls, fried onions, and lashings of ketchup.

Meatballs

Serves 4

Ingredients

2 tbs of oil
1 lb (500g) of minced beef
1 onion, peeled and finely chopped
3 slices of bread
1 dessert spoon of fresh chopped parsley
1 tsp of chilli powder

Remove the crusts from the bread, then tear into minuscule pieces. Those with a blender can give them a whizz for a few secs. Mix the breadcrumbs, mince, parsley, chilli powder and onion together and mould into a ball. Then heat the oil in a frying pan and fry your balls evenly for about 10 to 15 minutes, turning regularly. Don't make the balls too big or they will not be cooked in the middle.

Lamb and leek casserole

Serves 4

Ingredients

2 tbs of oil
4 lamb chops
1 onion, peeled and sliced
2 leeks, sliced
1/2 lb (250g) of carrots, scraped and chopped
4 oz (100g) of peas
1 pint (0.5 litre) of beef/vegetable stock
Salt
Pepper

Heat the oil in a frying pan then fry the chops for a couple of minutes on each side. Then add the onion, carrots and leek, and fry for a few more minutes. Transfer into a casserole dish, season, and pour the stock over. Put a lid on the dish and place in the oven on Gas Mark 4 (350 Deg F, 180 Deg C) for about 1 hour. Add the peas about 15 minutes before serving.

Tuna Mornay

Serves 4

Ingredients

4 hard boiled eggs
1 large tin of tuna
6 sliced tomatoes
1/2 pint (0.25 litre) of white sauce or cheese sauce
1 oz (25g) of grated cheese
Chopped parsley or watercress

Cut the eggs in half, lengthways. Mix the yolks with the tuna. Place the sliced tomatoes in a greased oven dish, then place the whites of the eggs on the tomatoes. Spoon the mixture of tuna and yolk onto the egg whites. Make the sauce according to the packet instructions or follow the recipes given in the chapter on **Dressings and sauces**, and pour the sauce over the mixture while it is hot. Sprinkle with grated cheese.

Place in a moderate oven at Gas Mark 6 (425 Deg F, 220 Deg C) for about 20 minutes until lightly browned. Garnish with parsley or watercress.

Hot chicken

Serves 4

Ingredients

4 pieces of chicken
1 onion, peeled and chopped
1 green pepper, seeded and chopped
2 tbs of oil
1 tin of tomatoes (14 oz)
3 tsp of chilli powder
Salt
Pepper

Heat the oil in a large saucepan and fry the onions for 3 to 4 minutes, then add the chilli powder, salt and pepper. Cook for another couple of minutes. Add the chicken and the pepper and cook for about 10 minutes. Then add the tomatoes and simmer for 40 minutes, adding a little water if the sauce begins to burn. Serve with rice.

Roast dinners

The traditional Sunday roast hasn't yet died out in our house, although it is more often served in the evening than at lunchtime. Those sharing a house will find it is good to make the effort to have a roast, as it makes a pleasant change from all the rushed meals that are grabbed between lectures during the rest of the week.

Remember that when using the oven, it should be switched on 20 minutes before the joint is put in to heat it up to the correct temperature.

Roast beef

Serves 2 to 20 (according to whether you have a small joint or a whole cow)

Ingredients

1 joint of beef
1/4 pint (125ml) of vegetable oil
Gravy
Salt
Pepper

Before throwing away the packaging for your joint, note how much it weighs. Allow 20 minutes cooking time per lb, plus 20 minutes on top, all at Gas Mark 7 (450 Deg F, 230 Deg C). This will allow for cooking the meat 'English style', ie with not too much blood seeping out. If you prefer it 'rare', cook for about 15 minutes less.

Put the joint in a roasting tin and pour the oil over the top and the sides. Season heavily with the salt and pepper, and stick in the oven.

The joint must be 'basted' - that means to spoon the oil in the tin over the top of the meat to stop it from drying out. Do this two or three times.

When the meat is cooked, carve the joint and serve with fresh vegetables. Gravy can be made from the juices in the roasting tin.

Roast pork

This must be cooked for a little longer than beef, for it is essential that pork is well cooked. Prepare in the same method as the beef but cook for 25 minutes per pound plus 25 minutes over, on the same oven setting. Baste the joint every 20 minutes. If you like garlic try sticking pieces of garlic in the joint before cooking.

Roast lamb

Lamb is still expensive but has a wonderful flavour that makes it worth splashing out on occasionally.

Prepare in the same method as the beef and cook for 20 minutes per pound and 20 minutes over on the same oven setting. Baste every 20 minutes.

Roast chicken

It is important not to overcook chicken as it loses all its flavour and is harder to carve.

Place the chicken in a baking tin with 1/4 pint of oil and season with plenty of black pepper and bake for 15 to 20 minutes per pound plus 20 minutes on Gas Mark 6 (425 Deg F, 225 Deg C).

Roast potatoes

Peel the potatoes and cut them in half if they are large. Boil the potatoes for 5 minutes in slightly salted water, then place them in the baking tray with the joint and baste them with the fat. Allow at least 60 minutes for them to cook.

Italian

For those who think of Italy only as the vague backdrop to *The Merchant of Venice* laboriously studied at school, think again. You haven't lived until you have discovered the wonders of Italy and its cuisine.

Choosing pasta

Pasta is probably one of the most widely used ingredients in Italian cooking and, like the French, Italians are not hesitant in the use of garlic and fresh herbs. The advantage of cooking with pasta is that there is almost no limit to what you can do with it. Obviously there are set rules and standard recipes, but personal experimentation is important and fun. Fresh pasta (as a friend commented, 'that soggy stuff in a packet') is now quite common, especially in the large supermarkets, although those on a grant will find it cheaper to use the dried variety.

After choosing between fresh and dried pasta there is also the decision as to what type to use. Pasta comes in a wide range of shapes and sizes, perhaps the most common being spaghetti. It can also be found in the shape of shells, quills, ribbons, twists, to name but a few. For those who have not outgrown tinned pasta you might be lucky enough to get space invaders, but I don't think that the Italians would approve of this.

Cooking pasta

Correct cooking of the pasta is essential. After the water has boiled add a pinch of salt. Long pasta like spaghetti should be eased gently into a pan making sure that it is not broken. Adding a couple of drops of olive oil can prevent sticking. The pasta should be cooked with the lid off, and stirred occasionally.

Normally, dried pasta requires 8 to 10 minutes in boiling water. Someone once told me that the best way to see if it is cooked is to throw a piece on the wall. If it sticks, it's ready. This occurred during a dinner party, and everybody decided to join in. Apart from making a mess on your wall this is not the most reliable way to test the pasta. While it should have some 'bite' to it (al dente), make sure that the pasta is not too undercooked, as this could result in indigestion (otherwise known as 'gut rot').

If you are cooking fresh pasta it normally only requires 2 or 3 minutes, so watch it carefully. If you overcook your pasta it will stick together and will taste very doughy.

The secret of getting a wonderful tasting sauce is to **reduce** it. This entails simmering the sauce until the liquid thickens and its volume reduces. When this happens the flavours are enhanced. If you have time let the sauce simmer for at least 20 minutes.

Basic tomato sauce (for pasta dishes)

Serves 3 to 4

Ingredients

2 tbs of olive oil/vegetable oil
1 large onion, peeled and chopped
2 cloves of garlic, peeled and finely chopped
1 tin of tomatoes (14 oz)
1 tbs of tomato puree
2 oz (50g) of Parmesan cheese or cheddar cheese
6 fresh basil leaves or 1 tsp of dried oregano
Salt
Pepper

Heat the oil in a saucepan, then add the chopped onion and garlic and fry gently for 3 to 4 minutes. When these have softened, add the tomatoes, puree, herbs, salt and pepper. Cook for another 20 minutes until they have been reduced, then add cheese if required.

Serve with a pasta of your choice.

Tomato and tuna sauce

This is one of my most used recipes when studying.

Serves 4

Ingredients

2 tbs of olive oil/vegetable oil
1 medium onion, peeled and chopped
1 clove of garlic, peeled and finely chopped
1 tin of tomatoes (14oz)
1 tbs of tomato puree
1 tin of tuna
1 tsp of oregano
1 tsp of brown sugar
Black pepper
Salt

Heat the oil in a medium sized saucepan and fry the onions and garlic for about 5 minutes. Then add the tomatoes, puree, oregano, salt, pepper, sugar and tuna. Simmer for about 20 minutes or until the sauce has been reduced. Serve with a pasta of your choice.

Spaghetti Bolognese

Most students have probably tried preparing this classic Italian dish at some point. There are many variations of the recipe, this is my preferred one.

Serves 4

Ingredients

2 tbs of oil
1 lb (500g) of minced beef

1 onion, peeled and chopped
1 tin of tomatoes (14 oz)
4 oz (100g) of mushrooms, washed and sliced
2 cloves of garlic, finely chopped
1 carrot, grated
2 rashes of bacon, cut into small pieces
Glass of red wine, optional
1 tbs of tomato puree
3/4 pint (350ml) of beef stock
2 tsp of oregano
Salt
Pepper

Put the oil in a large saucepan and heat, then add the onions and garlic, and fry gently for 5 minutes, being careful not to burn them. Add the minced beef and continue frying for a further 10 minutes. Then add the other ingredients.

After your sauce has reduced, which takes around 20 minutes, serve with a pasta of your choice - it doesn't have to be spaghetti.

Tomato and ham pasta sauce

Serves 4

Ingredients

2 tbs of olive/vegetable oil
1 tin of tomatoes (14 oz)
1 onion, peeled and chopped
4 slices of ham, cut into strips
2 cloves of garlic, peeled and finely chopped
1 tbs of tomato puree
1 glass of red wine, optional
Salt

Pepper
2 tsp of oregano/mixed herbs

Heat the oil in a saucepan and fry the onions and garlic for about 5 minutes. Then add the other ingredients and simmer for 20 minutes. Serve with a pasta of your choice, topped with Parmesan or cheddar cheese.

Carbonara

I'm not sure if this is the traditional recipe for the dish, but it tastes good to me.

Serves 3 to 4

Ingredients

2 tbs of oil
2 mugs of pasta quills/shells
1 clove of garlic, peeled and finely chopped
4 rashers of streaky bacon, cut into small pieces
3 egg yolks, beaten
2 oz (50g) of grated Parmesan cheese
3 tbs single cream
Lots of fresh black pepper
A pinch of salt

Boil the pasta in a saucepan for about 15 minutes. 5 minutes before the pasta is cooked, fry the bacon in the oil for 4 to 5 minutes. When the pasta is cooked, strain, and add to the bacon. Then add the cheese, egg, cream and seasoning. Heat until the egg has cooked, stirring constantly (this should take just a couple of minutes), then serve immediately with more black pepper.

Pasta with courgette and bacon sauce

If you don't have any bacon, slices of ham could be used.

Serves 4

Ingredients

2 tbs of olive/vegetable oil
1 onion, peeled and chopped
1 clove of garlic, peeled and finely chopped
1 tin of tomatoes (14 oz)
1 tbs of tomato puree
2 rashers of bacon, cut into strips
2 courgettes thinly sliced
2 tsp of oregano/herbes de Provence
Salt
Pepper

Heat the oil in a large saucepan, then add the onion and garlic. Fry for about 3 or 4 minutes, then add the bacon and courgettes. Continue cooking for another 5 minutes, but don't have the heat up too high otherwise the onion will start to burn. A tablespoon of water can be added to help the cooking and to prevent any burning.

When the courgettes have softened add the tomatoes, puree, seasoning and the herbs. Simmer the sauce for at least 15 to 20 minutes then serve with pasta and Parmesan or grated cheddar on top.

Lasagne

This is one of everybody's favourite Italian dishes. See the vegetarian section for an alternative recipe.

Serves 4

Ingredients

2 tbs of oil
1 large onion, peeled and chopped
2 cloves of garlic, peeled and finely chopped
1 lb (500g) of minced beef
1 tin of tomatoes (14 oz)
1/4 pint (125ml) of beef stock
2 tbs of tomato puree
2 tsp of oregano
Salt
Pepper
1 packet of lasagne (no pre-cooking type)

For the sauce:

1 oz (25g) of butter
2 oz (50g) of flour
1 pint (0.5 litre) of milk
6 oz (150g) of cheese, grated

After heating the oil in a saucepan add the onion and garlic and cook for 5 minutes. Add the mince and cook thoroughly. Then add the tomatoes, oregano, beefstock, tomato puree and seasoning. After bringing to the boil, an optional simmering for 15 to 20 minutes will improve the flavour.

While the meat sauce is reducing, prepare the cheese sauce. Melt the butter in a saucepan and then add the flour, stirring constantly. Remove from the heat and add the milk in stages. If the milk is added in one go, you end up with lumps (in the sauce). After adding the milk, bring to the boil and add the cheese, saving a bit for the top. Then simmer for 3 or 4 minutes; the sauce should now begin to thicken.

OK, so your sauce has not thickened: don't panic! Try adding a bit more flour, but sieve if first if you can. Lumpiness can be rectified by pouring the mixture through a sieve.

Find a shallow baking dish and grease it, then add a layer of meat sauce followed by a layer of lasagne, followed by a layer of cheese sauce. Continue this formation until you have used up your mixtures, making sure you finish with the cheese sauce. As well as sprinkling cheese on top, fresh tomato can be added.

Bake on the middle shelf of a pre-heated oven at Gas Mark 6 (425 Deg F, 220 Deg C) for 30 to 40 minutes.

Macaroni cheese with tomato

This another of my favourite recipes. If you don't have any macaroni try using pasta shells.

Serves 4

Ingredients

4 oz (100g) of macaroni
6 oz (150g) of grated cheddar cheese
2 large tomatoes
3/4 pint (350ml) of milk
1 oz (25g) of flour or cornflour
1 oz (25g) of butter

Melt the butter in a saucepan and mix in the flour, then gradually add the milk, stirring constantly to avoid lumps. Bring to the boil, add the cheese, then leave to simmer for 3 to 4 minutes.

Now cook the macaroni according to the instructions on

the packet. When this is done, drain and mix with the cheese sauce. Put into a baking dish, top with sliced tomatoes and more cheese, and then grill until browned.

Pizza

Huge scope for variety here, both in toppings and bases. The easiest to make is the French bread pizza, because the base is simply a sliced baguette. Dough bases can be bought ready-made, but they cost more than French sticks or home-made doughs. Also, using Ragu or Dolmio for the topping saves a lot of time, but it is cheaper to make your own.

French Bread Pizzas...

Pizza Margherita

This is the basic pizza. If you want to design your own, use this and add your own toppings.

Serves 1

Ingredients

1 stick of French bread
Ragu/tomato puree
1 tsp of olive oil
1 oz (25g) of grated cheese
Pinch of oregano
Pepper

Slice the french stick in half and spread some tomato puree on top. A thin layer will do - if you put too much on your pizza will become soggy. Place the cheese on top, season, add the herbs and pour on the oil. Bake in the oven until the cheese turns a golden brown colour. It should take roughly 15 minutes on Gas Mark 7 (450 Deg F, 230 Deg C), or until the cheese turns golden brown.

Pizza Roma

Serves 1

Ingredients

1 stick of French bread
Ragu/tomato puree
1 tsp of oil
1 oz (25g) of grated cheese
2 oz (50g) of tuna
2 to 3 onion rings
Pinch of oregano
Pepper

Spread some tomato puree on the bread. Place the tuna on first, then the onion rings and finally the cheese. Season, add the oregano and oil and cook as above.

Pizza Rialto

Serves 1

Ingredients

A 10 inch slice of French bread
Ragu/tomato puree
1 slice of ham
2 medium sized mushrooms, washed and
sliced
1 oz (25g) of grated cheese
1 tsp of oil
Pinch of oregano
Pepper

Spread some tomato puree on the bread, then add the ham. If the slice is to large, cut into a more usable size. Add a layer of mushrooms and cover with cheese. Season, add the oregano and cook as above.

Flat pizzas...

Pizza Face

Recommended recipe for Art students - try to make the face resemble someone you know, bearing in mind the limitations of a tomato eyes and nose, and green pepper eyebrows and mouth.

Serves 1

Ingredients

Ragu/tomato puree
Tomato, sliced in two
1 tsp of oil
3 oz (75g) of grated cheese
Pinch of oregano
Green pepper, seeded and sliced
Pizza base mix
Salt
Pepper

Mix the pizza base according to the instructions on the packet, then spread on a thin layer of tomato puree. Sprinkle on the cheese, season, pour on the oil, then make a face using the tomato and green pepper. Bake in the oven for 15 to 20 minutes at Gas mark 7 (450 Deg F, 230 Deg C) or until golden brown.

There is almost no limit to what you can put on a pizza. Here is a list of suggested toppings that can be used as a basis for designing your own.

- **Ham**
- **Pepperoni**
- **Tuna**
- **Mushrooms**
- **Onions**
- **Green peppers**
- **Red peppers**
- **Fresh tomato**
- **Spinach**
- **Egg**
- **Olives**
- **Sultanas**
- **Leeks**
- **Capers**
- **Anchovies**
- **Hot green chilli peppers**
- **Pineapple**
- **Sweetcorn**
- **Exotic cheeses**
- **Prawns**
- **Tandoori chicken**

To see how it's done properly, visit your local Pizza Express restaurant. There is a list of their branches at the back of this book.

Italian chicken risotto

Risotto dishes are ideal for students because they are filling, cheap and easy to prepare. Although this recipe uses chicken it can be made with ham or liver.

Serves 4

Ingredients

**1 oz (25g) of margarine
1 onion, peeled and chopped
1 clove of garlic, peeled and finely chopped
3 oz (75g) of chicken, cut into pieces
8 oz (200g) of rice
2 oz (50g) of mushrooms
1 pint (0.5 litre) of chicken stock**

Heat the margarine in large a saucepan and fry the chicken pieces for 5 minutes, then remove from the pan and put them in a bowl.

Fry the onion and garlic for 3 to 4 minutes. Put the rice in a sieve and wash under cold water to remove the starch. Then add the rice to the onions and fry gently for a couple more minutes.

Prepare the stock using boiling water, then add a third of it to the saucepan. After the stock has been absorbed by the rice add the rest of the stock and simmer until the rice is cooked.

When the rice is cooked add the chicken and mushrooms and cook for a minute or so, to heat them through.

Batchelors

Pasta 'n' Sauce

Batchelors
Pasta 'n' Sauce is
easy to prepare and
flexible enough to fit in with a busy student
lifestyle.

Enjoy it on its own, as an accompaniment or why not try one of the quick and easy on-pack recipe suggestions.

Chilli Chicken au Gratin

Servings: 2 — Preparation: 15 mins — Cooking: 20 mins

Ingredients

1 packet Chicken & Mushroom Pasta 'n' Sauce

1 dessertspoon vegetable oil

1 chicken breast, diced

1 courgette, sliced

198g (7 oz) can sweetcorn, drained and juice reserved

2 pineapple rings, chopped

1/2 - 1 tablespoon chilli sauce

Salt and black pepper

Topping:

50g (2 oz) Cheddar cheese, grated

3 tablespoons breadcrumbs

Method of Preparation

1. Make up the Pasta 'n' Sauce according to the pack instructions but only simmer for 10 minutes.

2. Heat the oil in a frying pan and fry the chicken for 3 minutes. Add the courgette and fry for a further 2-3 minutes, stirring continuously.

3. Add the Pasta 'n' Sauce with the pineapple, chilli sauce and seasoning to taste. Simmer for 5 minutes.

4. Place in ovenproof dish and sprinkle with the topping ingredients. Place under a hot grill until golden brown.

Quick & Easy

Batchelors

SOUPS

Make cooking quick and easy using Batchelors Soups. There are lots of tasty varieties to choose from, many of which have the Vegetarian Society seal of approval.

Why not enjoy a bowl of tasty Batchelors soup with crusty bread or be adventurous and try one of the on-pack recipes.

Creamy Vegetable Risotto
Servings: 3-4

Ingredients

1½ pt packet Batchelors Broccoli & Cauliflower Soup

10ml (2 teaspoons) oil

15g (½ oz) butter

1 medium onion, chopped

1 clove garlic, crushed

225g (8 oz) risotto or long grain rice

3 tablespoons frozen mixed vegetables

850ml (1½pt) water

Grated rind and juice of ½ lemon

Method of Preparation

1. Heat the oil and butter in a non-stick saucepan. Add the onion and garlic and cook until soft, stirring occasionally.

2. Add the rice and cook for 2 minutes, stirring.

3. Add the remaining ingredients and bring to the boil, stirring. Cook gently for about 20 minutes, stirring frequently, until the rice is just tender and the mixture is thick and creamy.

French

The French like to think of themselves as producing the best lovers, the finest wines, and the Citroen 2CV. In spite of this, the French can produce food which is extremely palatable, especially when washed down with a few litres of Beaujolais, and their only major fault for some is the use of large amounts of garlic. Residents of Dover often complain that the smell of garlic wafts over the Channel on windy days. Either the French have a serious vampire problem, or they genuinely have a taste for the stuff.

French food in English restaurants has a good reputation, but can often be a bit fancy and expensive. Luckily, though, many French dishes that are wonderfully simple and a gastronomic delight are easy to recreate at home.

The French influence on my cooking comes from the more provincial style of cooking.

Chicken in beer

The temptation is always to leave out the chicken from this recipe, but aim for restraint.

Serves 4

Ingredients

2 tbs of oil
4 chicken pieces
1 onion, peeled and chopped
3 carrots, scraped and chopped
1 leek, sliced
4 oz (100g) of mushrooms, sliced
1 large can of your favourite lager/ale
Salt
Pepper

Put the oil in a casserole dish, then fry the onion for 3 to 4 minutes, add the chicken and fry for another 10 minutes. Chuck the rest of the ingredients in the dish then stick in the oven for 1 hour on Gas Mark 5 (400 Deg F, 200 Deg C).

Then drink the rest of the beer, taking care not to get so drunk that you forget to take the chicken out of the oven.

Pork Provençal

I have an affinity for the Provence region of France that rivals even that of Peter Mayle - if I make enough money one day, I hope to be able to rent a Provencal cowshed from him, and thus be able to retire where the countryside is rugged and mountainous, the soil is dry and often unproductive, but the combination of great food, generous people and a lifestyle more laidback than the Tower of Pisa make it a number one holiday destination.

Over the years I have got to know the owners of a number of restaurants in rural Provence, and I am always impressed with the enthusiasm with which they prepare delicious and original meals for endless hoards of ungrateful holiday-makers. A four course meal can be bought for as little as the equivalent of £5. It is a shame that the quality and price of these meals cannot be reciprocated in Grand Bretagne.

This recipe is based on one of the fine offerings of Hotel du Commerce, Castellane, (they also make a mouthwatering chocolate mousse).

Serves 4

Ingredients

4 pork steaks/chops
1 onion, chopped and peeled
1 clove of garlic, peeled and finely chopped
1 tin of tomatoes (14 oz)
1 red pepper, cored and finely chopped
Salt
Fresh black pepper
2 tsp of herbes de Provence
1 finely chopped courgette
4 slices of cheddar cheese
2 tbs of oil

Fry the onion and garlic in the oil for about 5 minutes. When these have cooked, add the tomatoes, red pepper, courgette, herbs and seasoning. Let the sauce simmer for 20 minutes. After 10 minutes, grill the pork on foil, turning occasionally, and when it is nearly cooked put some sauce and the slices of cheese on the pork and grill until the cheese begins to melt.

Note that thinner pork chops will take less cooking time. Serve with potatoes and fresh vegetables and the rest of the sauce.

Lemon chicken

This recipe is a refreshing change to the more common ways of presenting chicken.

Serves 4

Ingredients

2 tbs of olive oil/vegetable oil
4 chicken pieces, preferably breast

Juice of 1 lemon
Fresh black pepper

Cut the chicken into small pieces (this allows the lemon to flavour a larger area). Heat the oil in large frying pan then add the chicken, lemon juice and pepper. Fry for 5 minutes, or until the chicken is cooked all the way through, adding more lemon juice before serving, if required.

Serve with a salad and pitta or French bread.

Chicken in wine

This recipe uses only one glass of wine, so if you have a bit left over from last night's booze-up, use that.

Serves 4

Ingredients

4 chicken pieces
1 glass of red or white wine
2 onions, peeled and chopped
1/2 pint (0.25 litre) of vegetable stock
2 tbs of flour
2 tbs of oil
Pepper
Salt

Put the flour in a dish and roll the chicken in it until they are evenly covered. Heat the oil in a large saucepan then fry the onions for 5 minutes or until they are golden. Then fry the chicken pieces for another 5 minutes. Add the stock, onions, seasoning and of course the wine, and simmer for 45 minutes.

Pork Normandy

Serves 4

Ingredients

2 tbs of oil
4 pork chops
1 tin of pineapple slices in natural juice
1 chicken stock cube
1 small apple, cored and chopped
1 small onion, peeled and chopped
Salt
Pepper

Heat the oil in a frying pan and then fry the chops for 3 to 4 minutes on each side, then put in an ovenproof dish. Add the onion and the apple. Make up the stock using 3/4 pint (375ml) of water, and add the juice of the pineapple. Pour this over the chops, season, then cover the dish with foil, and cook in the oven for 3/4 hour at Gas Mark 4 (350 Deg F, 180 Deg C). Then add the pineapple and cook for a further 15 minutes or until the chops are tender.

Chicken with mushrooms and peppers

Serves 4

Ingredients

2 tbs of vegetable/olive oil
4 chicken pieces, breast, leg, thigh, etc
1 green pepper, seeded and sliced into rings
4 oz (100g) of mushrooms, washed and sliced
1 pint (0.5 litre) of chicken stock
1 onion, peeled and chopped
Salt
Pepper

Heat the oil in a medium sized saucepan, then fry the onions and chicken for about 5 minutes. Add the mushrooms, peppers and seasoning and continue frying for another 10 minutes. Pour the chicken stock over the top and simmer for 30 minutes. Serve with potatoes or rice.

Quiche

For this recipe an 8 inch (20cm) flan dish and a rolling pin are needed.

Once the basic technique of making a quiche is mastered, limitless combinations of this classic French dish can be produced. Many people are put off preparing a quiche because it involves making pastry, but it is not as hard as it sounds.

Short crust pastry

Ingredients for pastry

8 oz (200g) of plain flour
2 oz (50g) of lard
2 oz (50g) of margarine/butter
2/3 tbs of water
A pinch of salt

This is perhaps one of the only times when I would make the effort to sieve the flour and salt, but don't worry if you don't possess such an implement. After sieving the flour and the salt add the lard and butter. It is easier to rub in if the fat is cut into little cubes.

The term 'rubbing in' is the procedure in which, using the fingertips, the flour and the fat are combined to produce a consistency of fine bread crumbs.

After rubbing in, add some water a little at a time. The water is needed to bind the mixture together, but be careful not to add enough to make the pastry become sticky. Mould the pastry into a ball then roll out on a floured board or very clean floured work surface. Also sprinkle a coating of flour onto the rolling pin. The flour is used to stop the pastry from sticking to the board and the pin.

Roll the pastry so that its area is big enough to cover the flan dish, then carefully place the pastry over the dish and mould it in the shape of the dish. Remove the edge of the overlapping pastry by running a knife along the rim of dish.

The next stage is to make the filling of the quiche.

Quiche Lorraine

Serves 4

The most famous quiche of all has to be the Lorraine. Its name derives from its region of origin, and is delicious eaten hot or cold. Unfortunately I have had to bastardize this recipe slightly by cutting out the cream as this makes it rather expensive for students. But if you are feeling flush then half the milk can be substituted for single cream: it's well worth it.

Ingredients for filling

4 eggs
1/2 pint (0.25 litre) of milk
4 oz (100g) of bacon
Salt
Pepper
2 oz (50g) of cheese, optional

Cut the bacon into small pieces, then fry lightly for a couple of minutes and place on the bottom of the pastry base. Beat the eggs together, add the milk, season and beat again. Pour over the bacon, sprinkle the cheese on top if required and bake in a hot oven Gas Mark 6 (425 Deg F, 220 Deg C), for 25 minutes or until the filling has set.

Alternative fillings can be used - try creating your own. This is another popular combination...

Cheese and onion

Another delicious quiche filling. Nicer than a tooth filling, anyway.

Ingredients for filling

1 tbs of oil
4 eggs
1/2 pint (0.25 litre) of milk
4 oz (100g) of grated cheddar cheese
1 onion, peeled and chopped
Salt
Pepper

Heat the oil in a frying pan, then lightly fry the onions for a couple of minutes. Place the onion on the bottom of the pastry case. Beat the eggs together, add the milk, season and beat again. Pour over the onion, sprinkle the cheese on top, then bake in a hot oven on Gas Mark 6 (425 Deg F, 220 Deg C), for 25 minutes or until the filling is cooked.

Oriental

Too often Oriental cuisine is thought of as fried lice and a bit of chop suey served in a foil carton. This is not the true taste of the Orient, but unfortunately it is not always possible to find a decent and uncliched menu. With the availability of fresh oriental produce in most supermarkets, many people have taken to home experimentation.

We'll just stick to home cooking, though.

Baked fish with ginger

Serves 1 to 2, depending on size of fish

Ingredients

1 whole fish, cleaned
1 clove of garlic, peeled and finely chopped
1 tsp of soy sauce
Juice of 1 lemon
1 oz (25g) of fresh ginger, peeled and thinly sliced
Tin foil

Place the fish on a piece of foil. Mix the lemon juice, soy sauce, garlic and ginger together and pour over the fish. Seal the fish up in the foil and bake in the oven for 40 minutes at Gas Mark 5 (400 Deg F, 200 Deg C).

Stir fry

Those fortunate enough to possess a wok will find Oriental cooking a lot easier than those stuck with the indignity of a frying pan. If you do have to use a frying pan use the biggest one you have. The wok is one of my most used kitchen accessories -its use does not have to be confined to Oriental cooking.

It is up to you what to put in a stir fry, though it is often a good way of using up any spare vegetables that are lurking in the back of your cupboard and are undergoing a metamorphosis into a different life form.

Vegetable stir fry

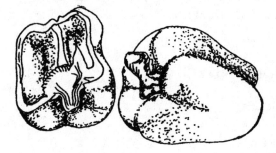

Serves 4

Ingredients

2 tbs of oil
1 red pepper, seeded and chopped
1 onion, peeled and chopped
1 green pepper, seeded and chopped
1 carrot, cut into thin strips
1 clove of garlic, peeled and finely chopped
1 tin of bamboo shoots
1 tin of water chestnuts
1 pack of fresh bean sprouts
2 tbs of soy sauce
Salt
Pepper

Pour the oil into your wok or frying pan, then when the oil is hot, ie when it is smoking (try not to set fire to the kitchen in the process), add the onion and garlic, and fry for 5 minutes. If you are using water chestnuts, cook these first as they take the longest to cook, and are nicer when they are slightly crispy. Then add the soy sauce, seasoning, and other vegetables except for the beansprouts.

After frying the vegetables for about 5 to 10 minutes, add the beansprouts and cook for a couple more minutes. It is important to keep the beansprouts firm: if they are overcooked. Serve with rice.

Economy stir fry

Serves 2 to 3

Ingredients

1 red pepper, seeded and chopped
1 onion, peeled and chopped
1 leek, sliced
2 carrots, scraped and cut into strips
A tub of beansprouts
2 tbs of oil
2 tbs of soy sauce
Black pepper
Salt

Heat the oil in a large frying pan or wok then fry the onions, leeks, carrots, seasoning, soy sauce and pepper for about 10 minutes. Then add the beansprouts and fry for a few more minutes.

Pork stir fry

Serves 2

Ingredients

**2 tbs of oil
1/2 lb (250g) of diced pork
1 green pepper, seeded and chopped
1 onion, peeled and chopped
2 tsp of chilli powder
1 clove of garlic, peeled and sliced
1 tbs of soy sauce**

Heat the oil in a large frying pan or wok, then fry the onions and the garlic for about 3 to 4 minutes. Add the pepper, soy sauce and the pork and fry until the pork is cooked. This should take about 10 minutes, depending on the size of the meat pieces. Serve with rice.

Coconut and chicken soup

This recipe is based on a dish that I had in a restaurant on a remote island in Thailand. The owner of the restaurant turned out to be French, and it was a somewhat strange experience to be eating freshly made croissants in a place where there were no cars, no roads, and not even any proper houses. I had some of the best meals in my life in MaMa's, even though the restaurant was hardly more than a tin shack. It is the quality of food, the friendliness of the service and the general ambience that can provide a perfect meal - not frilly tablecloths, crystal glasses and extortionate prices.

Serves 4

Ingredients

2 tbs of oil
3 chicken breasts
1 pint (0.5 litre) of water
3 oz (75g) of soluble coconut
1/2 tsp of curry powder
2 oz (50g) of fresh ginger
1 tsp of flour
4 tbs of cream, optional
Pepper
Salt

Remove the skin from the chicken if it still has one, then chop the chicken into bite sized pieces. Heat the oil in a large saucepan, and fry the chicken for about 5 minutes, turning frequently to stop it sticking to the pan.

Using a sharp knife remove the outer layer of the ginger and then slice it into thin pieces. Don't make the pieces too small as they are not recommended to be eaten. Add the ginger, curry powder, flour and seasoning to the chicken.

Dissolve the coconut in the water - it is easier if the water is hot. Add the coconut to the other ingredients, bring to the boil, then simmer for 15 to 20 minutes. The cream should be added 5 minutes before serving.

Serve the soup with a side order of rice.

Indian

Indian cuisine is probably the most fascinating area of cooking I have yet come across. I have only made one brief trip to India, but it's a country I will never forget and to which I am most keen to return. I would have liked to have had more time to learn about the different regional culinary influences, but my time there was limited.

At one guest house I was staying the cook seemed unable to deviate in any way from the theme of curry. In fact everything tasted of curry, be it tea, an omelette or a curry. Even our laundry was returned with the subtle aroma of curry.

Indian cooking for most people is simplified by using ready prepared curry powders. This, although it will undoubtedly produce a curry, will not represent the true flavour of India. Purists will know that the secret of Indian gastronomy is in the use of a vast combination of different spices and flavourings. I am not saying you can't make a good curry without these spices, but they certainly make a difference to the taste.

It is unfortunate that some people seem to just try and produce the hottest curry they can by shovelling in a tin of curry powder and a dozen chillies, so they can impress their friends with their machismo. The idea of curry is to produce a combination of flavours and tastes that harmonise together, not to produce a vile discord and numb your mouth into oblivion. The recipes in this section are fairly standard and do not require the use of anything too difficult to obtain.

If you share my passion for Indian food it is worthwhile reading some specialist Indian cookbooks. They will explain about the wide variety of spices available, and may have more exciting and original recipes than I can offer.

Vegetable curry

Curry is one dish that most students are familiar with, though not normally when in a state of complete consciousness. A four pack, a video and a vindaloo often make for an entertaining night in. But there is no need to waste valuable drinking money on a luke-warm, microscopic takeaway.

Half an hour in the kitchen could yield a curry that would last you and your mates a few days and still be cheaper than buying from the local Taj. There are literally thousands of different recipes for curry, but a vegetable curry is both amazingly cheap and about as suited for freezing as the South Pole. So why not make a bit extra and save it for when the grant runs out mid-term?

Serves 4

Ingredients

4 potatoes, diced into 1 inch (2.5cm) cubes
1 sliced leek
1 tin of tomatoes (14 oz)
2 sliced courgettes
1 onion, peeled and chopped
2 cloves of garlic, peeled and finely chopped
1 small pot of natural yoghurt
1 tbs of madras curry powder
1 dried red chilli
1/2 pint (0.25 litre) of beef stock
Any spare vegetables
2 tbs of oil
1 to 2 tbs of water

Heat the oil in a large saucepan then fry the onion, garlic and curry powder for 5 minutes or until they have softened. Then add the other ingredients, except the yoghurt, bring to the boil, and simmer for 40 minutes or more. Add the yoghurt 5 minutes before serving.

Whilst the curry is simmering taste it to see if it is to the strength required. If it is not hot enough for your asbestos-lined mouth just add more curry powder. Serve with rice - if you can afford it use pilau or basmati rice.

Chicken curry

Serves 4

Ingredients

2 tbs of oil
4 chicken pieces
2 onions, peeled and chopped
2 cloves of garlic, peeled and finely chopped
3 tsp of curry powder
1 tsp of garam masala
2 fresh green chilli peppers, chopped into rings
1 tin of tomatoes (14 oz)
3 whole green cardamon pods
2 tbs of freshly chopped coriander
1 small pot of natural yoghurt
1 to 2 tbs of water

Heat the oil in a large saucepan, then fry the onion and garlic gently for 5 minutes or until they have softened. Add the curry powder, garam masala and chillies, and fry for a couple more minutes. Add the chicken and water and fry for 5 minutes. After this the other ingredients can be added, apart from the yoghurt, which is added 5 minutes before serving. Simmer for 30 to 40 minutes, then serve with rice.

Curried eggs

Serves 4

Ingredients

4 eggs
1 onion, peeled and finely chopped
4 tomatoes, finely chopped

3 tsp of curry powder
1/3 pint (200ml) of water
2 tsp of tomato puree
A small pot of natural yoghurt
1 oz (25g) of margarine
Salt
Pepper

Place the eggs in a saucepan with some water and boil for 8 minutes. While the eggs are boiling put the margarine in a frying pan and fry the onions with the curry powder for 5 minutes. Then stir in the tomatoes, tomato paste, salt, pepper, flour and the water. Bring to the boil, then simmer for 10 to 15 minutes. Peel the eggs then cut them in half and add them to the curry with the yoghurt. Simmer for another 5 minutes then serve with rice.

Cucumber Raita

If the roof of your mouth is feeling like a furnace, this might help. Cucumber raita is a side dish that is very refreshing and simple to prepare.

Serves 2 to 4

Ingredients

1/2 cucumber, peeled and chopped into pieces
A small pot of natural yoghurt
1 tbs of olive oil
1 tbs of freshly chopped mint
Pepper
Salt

Mix the cucumber, yoghurt and mint together in a bowl, pour the oil on top, and season.

Chicken Tandoori

Making your own tandoori will cost much less than buying from a takeaway or even a supermarket. This recipe can be eaten cold with salad.

Serves 4

Ingredients

4 chicken pieces - breast, thigh, wing
1 tbs of tandoori powder
1 clove of garlic, peeled and finely chopped
1/2 pint (0.25 litre) of plain unsweetened
natural yoghurt

Remove the skin from the chicken and make some small incisions in the flesh with a sharp knife - this is to allow the marinade to penetrate deep into the chicken.

Mix the garlic, tandoori powder and yoghurt together, then rub some of the mixture into the incisions. Leave the chicken in the marinade for at least 3 hours, turning occasionally. The longer it is left the more flavour it will gain.

Cook under a medium heat grill for about 20 minutes, spooning on some more marinade at the same time. Turn the chicken over every few minutes to prevent burning.

The chicken can also be eaten cold.

Greek

Although Stavros might have given Greek grub a bad reputation, don't be afraid of trying your local kebab shop. By the way, does anyone know whether those 12 inch chocolate eclairs are really made of cardboard?

Shish Kebab

This recipe uses no strange eclairs, concentrating instead on lamb marinated in yoghurt.

Serves 4

Ingredients

3/4 lb (375g) of lamb, cut into small cubes
1 pot of natural yoghurt
Juice of one lemon
1 tbs of olive oil
Salt
Pepper
Fresh rosemary

Prepare this meal well in advance, for the lamb has to marinate for at least a couple of hours in order to obtain its full flavour. Put the lamb in a bowl with the yoghurt, lemon juice, olive oil and seasoning. Stir well, then put the bowl in the fridge for a couple of hours, making sure the lamb is evenly coated in the marinade.

When ready to be cooked, divide the meat onto 4 skewers, place the rosemary on the grill pan and grill on for 10 to 15 minutes, turning the kebabs occasionally so they cook evenly. If there is any spare marinade use it to flavour the meat while it is being grilled.

Serve with salad and pitta bread.

Moussaka

Serves 4

Ingredients

1 large aubergine, sliced (that's a purplish
marrow)
2 onions, peeled and chopped
1 tin of tomatoes (14 oz)
1 tbs of tomato puree
1 clove of garlic, crushed and finely chopped
1 lb (500g) of minced beef or lamb
2 tbs of oil
1 oz (25g) of butter
1 oz (25g) of flour
3/4 pint (375ml) of milk
4 oz (100g) of grated cheese
Salt
Pepper

Heat a tablespoon of oil in a frying pan and fry the
aubergines until they are soft. Then place on a piece of
kitchen towel to absorb the fat. Put some more oil in the
frying pan if needed and fry the onions, garlic, and meat.
After about 10 minutes season, and add the tomatoes and
puree.

Grease a casserole dish with either butter or oil, and fill
it with alternate layers of aubergine and meat, finishing
with a layer of aubergine.

To make the cheese sauce, melt the butter in a saucepan,
add the flour, and mix together. Remove from the heat, and
very gradually add the milk. Boil until the sauce thickens,
then remove from the heat and add 3 oz (75g) of the cheese.
Pour the cheese sauce over the top of the aubergine, and
sprinkle the rest of the cheese on top. Bake for 40 minutes
on Gas Mark 5 (200 Deg C, 400 Deg F).

Hungarian

I'm afraid I don't know much about Hungary, except that they make Goulash. Hope you like it!

Goulash

This dish traditionally uses veal, but beef is normally used due to the controversy surrounding the methods by which veal is produced.

Serves 4

Ingredients

2 tbs of oil
1 large onion, peeled and chopped
1 lb (500g) of potatoes, peeled and sliced
1 clove of garlic, peeled and finely chopped
1 lb (500g) of cubed stewing beef
1 red pepper, seeded and chopped
1 green pepper, seeded and chopped
1/2 tsp of caraway seeds
1 tbs of paprika
1 tsp of mixed herbs
1 beef stock cube
3/4 pint (375ml) of boiling water
Salt
Pepper
4 oz (100g) of sliced mushrooms
1 tin of tomatoes (14 oz)
5 fluid oz (125ml) of soured cream, optional

Heat the oil in a casserole dish or a large saucepan, then fry the onions and garlic for a couple of minutes. Add the meat, peppers, tomatoes, paprika, caraway seeds, salt and pepper, and cook for about 5 minutes.

Dissolve the stock cube in the boiling water and add to the above. Simmer for about 40 minutes, then add the potatoes and cook for another 40 minutes. After about 30 minutes add the mushrooms. If they are added any earlier they will be overcooked and go mushy.

Before serving add the soured cream, if required.

Chicken paprika

Serves 4

Ingredients

4 chicken portions, skinned
1 clove of garlic, peeled and finely chopped
2 large onions, peeled and chopped
2 tbs of oil
5 fluid oz (125 ml) of soured cream
1 tbs of paprika
1/4 pint (125ml) of chicken stock
Salt
Pepper

Heat the oil in a casserole dish and fry the onions and garlic slowly for about 5 minutes. Add the chicken and paprika and continue to fry for a few minutes. Season, add the stock, and simmer for 30 minutes.

Just before serving stir in the soured cream. Serve with rice or potatoes.

Russian

Famed for its caviar and vodka, the latter of which tends to be more popular in student circles. The recent opening of a McDonald's store in Moscow has enabled Russians finally to savour a taste of western culture. And it is such a bargain - for the average Russian a Big Mac will only set them back a year's wages. So it is hardly surprising that the Russians have instead learnt to do 101 things with a potato. In fact, potatoes are their staple diet. So here is a recipe without them.

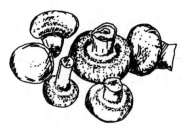

Beef Stroganov

This recipe traditionally uses fillet steak, but it is unlikely that you will be able to afford it, so rump or even stewing steak could be used as a substitute.

Serves 4

Ingredients

1 lb (500g) of steak
1 large onion, peeled and chopped
1 clove of garlic, peeled and finely chopped
4 oz (100g) of mushrooms, sliced
A glass of white wine
2 oz (50g) of butter
Salt
Pepper
1/2 pint (0.25 litre) of soured cream

Bash the steak with a rolling pin to flatten it out, but don't get too carried away. Then cut into strips 1/2 inch (1.5cm) wide and 2 inches (2.5cm) long. Fry the steak in the butter for about 3 or 4 minutes, then remove from the pan and put in a bowl.

Fry the onions and garlic, for 5 minutes, then add the mushrooms and cook until they have softened. Stir in the wine, season, and put the meat back. Cook for about 20 to 30 minutes, stirring occasionally to prevent burning.

Before serving, add the soured cream and heat through. Do not allow to boil, otherwise the cream will curdle.

Mexican

The atmospheric temperature is reflected in the food (it's damn hot) and can result in severe aromatic expulsions from the trasero. Mexican food is becoming increasingly popular as is the pretentious lager that is now served in most pubs. But these fads have a habit of disappearing as fast as they appeared.

Chilli con carne

This tends to go down with students almost as well as a pint of beer. The chilli can be made as hot as required, but remember that even though you may love to sweat, your housemates might prefer it a little milder. It can be served with rice, potatoes or pitta bread. Chilli tastes pretty good even when cold, and it has been known for me to dig into the leftovers for breakfast. I usually add a green or red pepper.

Serves 4

Ingredients

2 tbs of oil
3 tsp of chilli powder
1 lb (500g) of minced beef
1 large onion, peeled and chopped
2 cloves of garlic, peeled and finely chopped
1/4 pint (125ml) of beef stock
1 tin of tomatoes (14 oz)
1 tin of kidney beans, drained (15 oz)
1 tsp of oregano
1 tbs of tomato puree
Salt
Pepper
Glass of red wine, optional

After frying the onions, chilli powder and garlic in the oil for about 5 minutes, add the mince. Cook the mince for about 10 minutes stirring, constantly to stop it burning. Add the other ingredients, except the kidney beans, varying the amounts of seasoning according to taste. Bring to the boil then simmer for about 20 minutes (the longer the better). 5 minutes before serving add the kidney beans.

Serve with rice or jacket potatoes.

Nachos

Serves 4

Ingredients

2 tbs of oil
2 tsp of chilli powder
1 large onion, peeled and chopped
1 tin of chopped tomatoes (14oz)
1 large bag of tortilla chips
4 oz (100g) grated cheese
1 tbs of tomato puree
1 green pepper, cored and finely chopped
Salt
Pepper

Heat the oil in a large saucepan, then fry the onion and garlic for about 3 to 4 minutes. Add the chilli powder and the green pepper and cook for another couple of minutes. Then add the tomatoes, tomato puree and seasoning and cook for about 15 minutes.

Whilst the sauce is cooking arrange the tortilla chips in a ceramic dish. When the sauce is ready, pour over the chips and finally cover with cheese. Then place under a hot grill until the cheese has melted - enjoy.

Indonesian

Indonesia consists of about 15 thousand islands, so the culinary traditions range from the absurd to the delightful. Bali has fantastic restaurants, specialising in suckling pig and duck. They have also been influenced by the large numbers of Australians that flock to Kuta beach to surf and to pose, so peanut butter sandwiches and jaffles are normally on the menu.

However, their attempts at cooking western grub are not always entirely successful. Pancakes, for example, will rarely come less than 2 inches thick, and have the consistency of a sponge.

I came across a chef who had been trained by one of the international hotels and now runs his own 5 table restaurant! After discovering this jewel of a restaurant and eating there most nights of the week, he offered me the opportunity of choosing a western meal. My companion and I, after much deliberating, decided on macaroni cheese and apple strudel. But having prepared these dishes the chef became unwell and had to give his assistant strict instructions on how to cook our meal.

My companion and I eagerly waited the arrival of our first taste of western food for a long time.

Unfortunately, he didn't quite get it right. Both dishes arrived so overcooked that they were practically inedible, and we didn't have the heart to tell the chef the next day what had happened to his hard work.

The extent of the western influence on these islands varies considerably. I was travelling during at the time of the football World Cup, and happened to be on an island on which football fever was as widespread as it was at home. The tranquillity of an Indonesian night where normally the only sound would come from bored mosquitoes buzzing in one's ear would be shattered at 3 am by locals, crowded around the television, screaming and cheering, and eating nasi goreng.

Nasi goreng

Nasi means rice in Indonesian, and goreng means fried. This dish is often eaten for breakfast...someone should really introduce them to rice krispies.

Serves 1

Ingredients

A cup of rice
2 tsp of chilli powder
1 tbs of oil
Salt

Boil some water in a saucepan, chuck in a pinch of salt, then cook the rice until it is soft in the middle. This should take about 15 to 20 minutes. When the rice is cooked strain it. Heat the oil in a frying pan then add the cooked rice and chilli powder. Fry for 5 minutes, stirring constantly. If it is now edible then you have done something wrong. Try adding some more chilli.

If you wish to turn your nasi goreng into nasi goreng istimewa, fry an egg and place on top of the rice.

Spanish

If when in Spain your diet has room to be a little more adventurous than a pint of Watneys Red Barrel and a bag of chips, there are such dishes as Fabada, Coccido and of course Paella which can be washed down by copious quantities of Sangria.

Paella

This is probably Spain's most renowned dish. It traditionally uses seafood like prawns and mussels, but as these make it expensive for the student they can be left out.

Serves 4 to 5

Ingredients

4 tbs of olive oil
2 onions, peeled and chopped
2 cloves of garlic, finely chopped
8 oz (200g) of rice
1 green pepper, seeded and cut into pieces
4 oz (100g) of frozen peas
4 tomatoes (seeds removed)
1 pint (0.5 litre) of chicken stock
4 chicken pieces
A pinch of saffron
4 oz (100g) of cooked mussels, optional
4 oz (100g) of peeled prawns

Heat half the oil in a large frying pan, or preferably a wok, then fry the onions and garlic for 3 to 4 minutes. Add the rice, saffron, tomatoes and stock, bring to the boil, then cook gently for 10 minutes.

Fry the chicken in a separate pan with the remaining oil for 10 minutes or until lightly browned. Then add the chicken to the rice, stir in the other ingredients, and simmer until the rice is cooked. Serve with lemon wedges.

Spanish omelette

As there are numerous variations on this meal, don't hold yourself back with what you add.

Serves 4

Ingredients

4 eggs
1 potato, cooked for 10 minutes and chopped
2 tomatoes, sliced
1 oz (25g) of peas
1 onion, peeled and chopped
Mixed herbs
Salt
Pepper

Beat the eggs, season, add the vegetables and pour into a flan dish. Bake at Gas Mark 6 (425 Deg F, 220 Deg C) for 15 to 20 minutes or until the mixture ceases to be runny.
   Serve with a green salad and a pair of maracas.

American

The American chefs are widely acclaimed to be some of the finest gardeners in the world, and their burger culture has inspired some of the greatest love poetry since Wordsworth. Burgers, hashbrowns, pancakes with maple syrup, peanut butter and jelly sandwiches: how can anyone dispute the position that American cuisine holds in the world?

There is actually a lot more to American cuisine than burgers and hotdogs. Americans love to eat, and this is generally reflected in their size, and their obsession with fitness. Some parts of America boast a fantastic array of homegrown food - the deep South, with places like New Orleans, produces some mouthwatering dishes. Unfortunately, I can't remember what they are.

Burgers

This traditional example of American fare has now become one of the world's most popular forms of laxative. Rumours of the true ingredients of all-American burgers range from factory-bred worms to horsemeat. But for this recipe we'll try beef for a change.

Makes 4 burgers

Ingredients

1 lb (500g) of minced beef
1 onion, peeled and finely chopped
2 oz (50g) of bread crumbs
2 fluid oz (50ml) of milk
Salt
Pepper

Throw all the ingredients in a bowl, mix together, and divide the mixture into 4 portions. Shape each portion into something that resembles a burger. Grill for about 4 or 5 minutes on each side on a medium grill, or until golden brown. To produce a more exotic burger try adding chopped garlic and herbs.

Jambalaya

This is perhaps one of the ultimate Cajun recipes. A friend of mine from Louisiana introduced me to this recipe a couple of years ago - she made it using sausages and chicken, although apparently back home she said they also add alligator. It sounded interesting, but they always seem to be out of alligator steaks in Sainsbury's whenever I ask, so you will have to make do with chicken etc.

The sausages that are used in Cajun cooking are different to the British banger. One of the most widely used is of the chorizo variety. These are available in England, but if you can't find any then ordinary sausages will do. It is important to remember that in most recipes the ingredients given are guidelines, and that a lack of one particular item should not preclude you from attempting that recipe (unless, of course, you're trying to make toast without any bread etc). But generally speaking be brave and make up your own variation or concoction.

Serves 4

Ingredients

2 tbs of oil
2 chicken breasts, cut into pieces
1/2 lb (250g) of sausage (chorizo if available)
1/2 lb (250g) of rice
1 onion, peeled and chopped
2 cloves of garlic, peeled and finely chopped
1 green pepper, seeded and chopped into pieces
2 sticks of celery, chopped
1 tsp of Cayenne pepper
Salt
Pepper
1 pint (0.5 litre) of vegetable/chicken stock

Heat the oil in a large saucepan or a wok. Fry the onions, garlic, sausage and chicken for about five minutes, then add the pepper and celery. Continue frying for another couple of minutes, then season and add the Cayenne pepper. Pour the stock over the top and bring to the boil.

When the stock is boiling add the rice and cook for roughly 20 minutes or until the rice is soft when pinched. Be careful not to overcook the rice.

Chicken Maryland

Serves 4

Ingredients

2 tbs of oil
4 oz (100g) of mushrooms, sliced
4 chicken pieces, breast, thigh, drumsticks
Flour
1 egg, beaten
White breadcrumbs
1/2 pint (0.25 litre) of chicken stock
Fried bananas

Dip the chicken pieces first in a little flour, then in the egg. Then season and roll it in the breadcrumbs. Put the chicken in a baking tin with the oil and roast for 20 to 30 minutes, basting occasionally, on Gas Mark 5 (400 Deg F, 200 Deg C).

While the chicken is cooking, a sauce needs to be made. Pour the chicken stock into a saucepan, mix one tablespoon of flour into it, then add the mushrooms. Simmer for 10 minutes.

When the chicken is cooked, serve with the sauce and fried bananas.

Australian

Our antipodean neighbours like nothing better than a barbecued kangaroo steak, washed down with the old amber nectar.

Pumpkin soup

Serves 4

Ingredients

1 1/2 lb (750g) of pumpkin flesh, cut into cubes
1/2 pint (0.25 litre) of milk
4 oz (100g) of butter
Salt
Pepper

Melt the butter in a saucepan, then fry the pumpkin until it is soft and mushy. Season, then add milk and put into a liquidiser for a minute. Put the liquid back into a saucepan and heat through, but do not boil.

Australian billy tea

Ingredients

Creek water
Tea leaves

Put one cup of water per person plus one extra into the billy can. Then boil vigorously with the lid off. Add one slightly heaped teaspoon of tea per person and boil for a couple more minutes.

Remove the billy can and stir with a eucalyptus twig. If you're sufficiently confident, swing the billy overarm in a circular motion 3 times (not advisable for children, but perfect for irresponsible students).

Must be drunk by the billabong with a jumbuck and a didgeredoo in ya tucker bag.

More fish

If a recipe uses a whole fish it will need cleaning. This does not mean give it a bubble bath - it means the head, gills and innards have to be removed. Normally fish come already 'cleaned', but, if they don't, ask the fishmonger to do it for you.

Choosing fish is important. Look for the following qualities:

(i) It should not smell.

(ii) The eyes should be bright and full. If the fish is not so fresh the eyes will be dull.

(iii) The gills should be slime-free, clean and shiny.

(iv) If you poke a fresh fish, the flesh will spring back up.

(v) A fish has no legs.

Frozen fish does not tend to have as full a flavour as fresh fish. It is, however, useful to keep a couple of cod fillets in the freezer as they can be cooked fairly quickly and easily.

Grilled fish

Serves 1

Ingredients

1 cod steak
Butter
Pepper
Salt

Brush the fish with a little butter, season, and grill for about 10 minutes, according to the size and thickness of the fish, turning occasionally.

If you like a bit more flavour, squeeze some lemon or lime juice on top. Serve with potatoes or rice and fresh vegetables.

Baked mackerel

Serves 2

Ingredients

2 mackerel
2 tsp of mustard
2 tsp of vinegar
2 tbs of water

Clean the mackerel, then score across two or three times on each side. Sprinkle with mustard, vinegar and water. Put the fish in a greased baking tin and bake for 15 to 20 minutes on Gas Mark 5 (400 Deg F, 200 Deg C).

Baked fish in wine

Don't forget the fish!

Serves 2

Ingredients

2 cod steaks
1 onion, peeled and cut into rings
1 glass of wine, red or white
Pepper
Salt

Put the fish and onions in a shallow baking dish, season, pour the wine over the top and bake in the oven for 35 minutes at Gas Mark 5 (400 Deg F, 200 Deg C).

Scotch Kedgeree

Serves 4

Ingredients

8 oz (200g) of rice
1 egg
1/2 lb (250g) of smoked haddock fillet
2 oz (50g) of butter or margarine
Pepper
Salt
Juice of 1 lemon

Cook the fish by baking it in the oven for 25 minutes. Then remove from the oven and 'flake fish', removing all bones and skin. Cook the rice in boiling water according to the instructions on the packet, which should roughly take 20 to 25 minutes.

Drain and rinse the rice in boiling water - this gets rid of most of the starch. Hard boil the egg by cooking for 10 minutes in boiling water. Then cool, shell and chop into pieces.

Melt the margarine in a saucepan and add the fish, then cook for 3 to 4 minutes to reheat it. Stir in the lemon juice, chopped egg, seasoning and rice and serve immediately. Garnish with fresh parsley and more egg, according to taste.

Baked trout

Serves 2

Ingredients

2 small trout, cleaned
1 onion, peeled and finely chopped

1 carrot, peeled and finely chopped
1 clove of garlic, peeled and finely chopped
1 oz (25g) of flaked almonds
Salt
Pepper
1/2 oz (15g) of butter

Melt the butter in a frying pan, then add the onion, carrot, and garlic. Fry for about 5 minutes. Place each trout on a piece of tin foil, making sure the foil is big enough to completely wrap the fish. Divide the vegetables between the two fish, placing the vegetables on the top and the sides of the fish, sprinkle with the almonds, season, then seal up the 'parcels'.

Bake in the oven for about 20 minutes or Gas Mark 5 (200 Deg C, 400 Deg F).

Serve with potatoes, rice or salad.

Cod and onion bake

Serves 4

Ingredients

4 pieces of cod or any white fish, according to overdraft size
1 large onion, peeled and sliced into separate rings
3 sliced tomatoes
2 oz (50g) of butter/margarine

This is an easy dish that should take no more than 5 minutes to prepare. Put the fish and onion in an ovenproof dish with the butter, and bake for 20 minutes on Gas Mark 5 (400 Deg F, 200 Deg C). Then add the sliced tomatoes and cook for a further 10 minutes.

Serve with potatoes and fresh vegetables.

Vegetarian

Over the past decade the interest in vegetarian food has escalated into the situation where it is usual for most people to eat certain meat-free recipes in their normal diet. The number of vegetarians is increasing, especially among the younger generations.

There are many reasons for becoming vegetarian. For many it is the killing of the animals that puts them off meat; some people can't afford meat, and for others it is part of a healthier diet. Whatever the reason it is a misconception that vegetarian cooking is boring. The people that say this are the sort of people that eat pie and chips every night and think that a courgette is some sort of American car.

Vegan or vegetarian?

A **vegetarian** is someone who excludes meat or meat and fish from their diet, but will often eat dairy products and even eggs. They object to animals being killed for food, and so will not eat parts of dead animals.

A **vegan** eats no animal products at all - not even those produced by living creatures. This rules out dairy butter and cheese etc.

Jacket potato

This is a traditional component of a student diet, probably due to its low cost and simplicity. It is important to use old potatoes - new ones are not suitable. This also applies to roast potatoes.

Ingredients

1 large potato

After viciously stabbing your potato with a sharp implement

(preferably a fork), bung in the oven for about 60 minutes on Gas Mark 7 (450 Deg F, 230 Deg C).

Test the potato with a skewer or a knife to see if it is cooked in the middle.

To make the potato more exciting different fillings can be added on top, like...

- Cheese
- Coleslaw
- Tuna and mayonnaise
- Fried egg
- Cottage cheese and chives

Jacket potato with cheese and onion

This is another way of cooking jacket potatoes, but it takes a little more time.

Ingredients

1 large potato
2 oz (50g) of cheddar cheese, grated
1 onion
1 tbs of milk
A nob of butter

Follow the instructions for the above recipe, except when the potato is cooked slice it in half and scoop out the potato with a teaspoon and put in a mixing bowl. Try not to make a hole in the skins because you'll need them later.

Add a tablespoon of milk and a nob of butter and mash. Cut the onion up into pieces and fry for 3 to 4 minutes. Add the onion to the potato and mix together. Then spoon back the potato into the jackets, cover with cheese and cook for another 15 minutes or so. If the cheese starts to burn cover the potato with a piece of tin foil.

Stuffed cabbage

This recipe serves two. Rabbits, that is.

Ingredients

6 large cabbage leaves
8 oz (200g) of spinach
6 oz (150g) of cooked rice
2 oz (50g) of butter
4 oz (100g) of grated cheddar cheese
1 egg yolk
1/2 pint (0.25 litre) of vegetable stock

First, cook the spinach in a little water for 5 minutes, then drain and put aside. Cook the cabbage leaves for about two minutes. Melt the butter and add the chopped onion together with the rice, spinach, cheese, and seasoning. Bind with the egg yolk.

When thoroughly mixed, put a heaped spoonful of it onto each of the leaves, and wrap it up into a parcel. Place the parcel in an ovenproof dish and pour the stock on top. Cover with foil and bake for 30 minutes at Gas Mark 4 (350 Deg F, 180 Deg C).

Lentil curry

Made famous by Neil and good for the student status.

Serves 2

Ingredients

4 oz (100g) of lentils soaked in cold water for 1 hour
1/2 pint (0.25 litre) of vegetable stock
4 carrots, scraped and chopped

1 onion, peeled and chopped
1 courgette, sliced
1 leek, sliced
1 tbs of curry powder
2 fresh tomatoes sliced

Boil the lentils for about 7 minutes and then strain. Heat the oil in a large saucepan, then fry the onions and curry powder for 5 minutes. Add the other vegetables and fry for another 5 minutes. Then add the stock and lentils, bring to the boil, then simmer for an hour. Serve with rice.

Leeks with cheese

Popular among the Welsh fraternity. Serves 4.

Ingredients

2 lb (1 kg) of leeks
4 oz (100g) of cheese
Salt
Pepper

Chop the ends of the leeks and use the whitish bit, then slice into rings about 1/2 inch (1.5cm) thick and wash to remove any grit. Boil in water for about 5 minutes then strain. Place in an ovenproof dish, season, cover with cheese, and grill until the cheese has melted..

Tomato and aubergine bake

Serves 4

Ingredients

2 tbs of oil
1 large aubergine, thinly sliced
2 onions, peeled and chopped
2 cloves of garlic, chopped
5 oz (125g) pot of natural yoghurt

1 tin of tomatoes (14 oz)
1 tbs of tomato puree
1 tsp of dried oregano
Salt
Pepper
3 oz (75g) of grated cheddar cheese
1 oz (25g) of white breadcrumbs

Heat the oil in a frying pan and add the aubergine slices. It is best to cook it in stages because only the bottom of the pan needs to be covered at any one time. Fry the aubergine until it has softened and slightly browned, then place on kitchen paper to absorb the oil. After cooking all the aubergine, remove and fry the onion and garlic for 5 minutes.

The next stage is to add the tomato, tomato puree, oregano and seasoning. Bring to the boil, then simmer for 10 minutes and stir in the yoghurt.

Using a greased ovenproof dish, arrange the aubergine and the tomato sauce in layers, in that order. Continue this until the top layer is of aubergine. Cover the top with breadcrumbs and cheese.

Bake at Gas Mark 4 (350 Deg F, 180 Deg C), for around 30 minutes. Serve with rice or potatoes.

Other vegetables can be added, such as peppers or courgettes.

Ratatouille

This traditional Provencal recipe can really be made from whatever vegetables are available. Tinned tomatoes are cheaper than buying fresh ones (except in the summer when fresh ones are more affordable).

The lemon is considered optional by some, but I believe it to be essential, though I must give credit to Jan Sitwell for the idea.

Serves 4

Ingredients

2 tbs of oil
1 tin of tomatoes (14 oz)
2 onions, peeled and finely chopped
2 cloves of garlic, peeled and finely chopped
1 small aubergine, chopped
1 red pepper, cored and chopped
1 courgette, thinly sliced
1 lemon, quartered
2 tsp of herbes de Provence
2 bay leaves
A glass of red wine, water or tomato juice,
optional
Pepper
Salt

While you are preparing the other vegetables place the pieces of aubergine on a plate and sprinkle them with salt. After preparing the vegetables, wash the aubergine pieces then dry them with kitchen paper. Heat the oil in a large saucepan. Fry the onions and garlic for about 5 minutes, then add the courgette, the aubergines and the peppers. Cook for about 5 minutes then add the tomatoes, the lemon, and the other ingredients. Bring to the boil and then simmer for 30 minutes.

Ratatouille can be served with almost anything - rice, baked potato, pitta bread etc. It can also be served cold.

Vegetable kebabs

Serves 2

Ingredients

1 green pepper, seeded and cut into pieces
1 courgette, cut into chunks

1 small onion, peeled and quartered
2 tomatoes, quartered
4 mushrooms, halved or quartered
Salt
Pepper
1 oz (25g) of butter

Thread all the vegetables onto a couple of skewers and daub them with butter, then grill for about 15 minutes. For a different flavour try adding a tablespoon of runny honey or a dash of soy sauce whilst grilling. Serve with rice.

Pasta with pine kernels and sultanas

This recipe is very easy to prepare and tastes wonderful, unless the wrong sort of oil is used.

Serves 4

Ingredients

8 tbs of olive oil
10 oz (250g) of pasta
2 cloves of garlic, peeled and finely chopped
2 oz (50g) of sultanas
2 oz (50g) of pine kernels

Cook the pasta of your choice according to the instructions on the packet. Drain the pasta and place in a serving bowl. Pour the oil over the pasta then stir in the garlic, pine kernels and sultanas. Season using lots of fresh ground pepper then serve immediately. Parmesan can be added on top if required.

Clare's nutty rice

This recipe is best cooked in a large wok, but a saucepan or a dustbin lid will do.

Serves 2 to 4

Ingredients

2 tbs of oil
2 cups of wholemeal rice
1 green pepper, seeded and chopped
1 small tin of sweetcorn
1 onion, peeled and chopped
1 oz (25g) of mushrooms, sliced
1 clove of garlic, peeled and finely chopped
4 oz (100g) of walnuts
1 vegetarian Oxo cube
Fresh parsley
Salt
Pepper

Heat the oil in a large frying pan or wok then fry the onions and garlic for between 4 and 5 minutes. Add the mushrooms, garlic, green pepper and sweetcorn and fry for another couple of minutes. Next add the uncooked rice and about four cups of water. Sprinkle Oxo cube over and stir frequently. Simmer for about 20 minutes, depending on the type of rice used. Add more water if necessary to stop the rice from drying out.

If the rice is soft when pinched then it is cooked. Add the walnuts a couple of minutes before removing from the heat. Flavour with salt and pepper.

Parsley and pasta

Serves 2

Ingredients

4 oz (100g) of wholemeal pasta shells
1 blob of butter or margarine

1 or 2 oz (25 or 50g) of cheddar cheese, grated
Lots of fresh parsley, roughly chopped
Salt
Pepper

Boil the pasta until it goes soft, then drain. Add the butter and allow it to melt. Add the salt, pepper, cheese and parsley, and toss until evenly distributed, then serve immediately.

Vegetable bake

Serves 4

Ingredients

2 tbs of oil
1 onion, peeled
1 clove of garlic
1 courgette
1 small tin of sweetcorn
1 tin of tomatoes (14 oz)
1 oz (25g) of mushrooms
2 oz (50g) of cheddar
2 slices of bread
1 vegetarian Oxo cube
Mixed herbs
Salt
Pepper
A slosh of red wine, if available

Pre-heat the oven to 150 Deg C (300 Deg F, Gas Mark 2). Slice the onion, garlic, courgette and mushrooms, then heat up some oil in a frying pan and lightly fry them for 5 minutes. Add the sweetcorn, tomatoes, seasoning and wine. Mix the Oxo cube with a cup of water and add to the pan, and simmer for about 10 minutes.

If there's a food processor around, use it to turn the bread to breadcrumbs. Otherwise just tear the bread into oblivion with your bare (but clean) hands. Then grate the cheese.

Pour the vegetables into a casserole dish and cover with breadcrumbs and cheese. Put into the oven for 10 to 20 minutes, until the breadcrumbs have gone crispy and the cheese has melted.

Alternatively, serve without breadcrumbs and cheese as a sauce for pasta or rice.

Lasagne

You can use a meat substitute with this recipe, called silken tofu. It sounds like a Greek island, but it tastes a bit better than that. If you can find some, prepare in the same way as the meat lasagne (see Italian), substituting the meat for tofu. Reduce the cooking time, though.

Serves 4

Ingredients

2 tbs of oil
1 large onion, peeled and chopped
1 red pepper, seeded and chopped
1 green pepper, seeded and chopped
1 clove of garlic, peeled and finely chopped
1 leek finely chopped
2 courgettes finely sliced
1 tin of tomatoes (14 oz)
2 tbs of tomato puree
2 tsp of oregano
Salt
Pepper
1 packet of lasagne (no pre-cooking required type)

For the cheese sauce:

1 oz (25g) of butter
2 oz (50g) of flour
1 pint (0.5 litre) of milk
6 oz (150g) of cheese, grated

Heat the oil in a large saucepan and add the onion and garlic. Cook for 5 minutes, then stir in the leek, peppers and courgette, fry gently for another 3 minutes or so. Then add the tomatoes, puree, oregano and seasoning, bring to the boil then simmer for a further 20 minutes. While the vegetable sauce is simmering prepare the cheese sauce.

Melt the butter in a saucepan and add the flour, stirring constantly. Remove from the heat and add the milk in stages. Then bring to the boil and add the cheese, saving a bit for the top. Simmer for 3 or 4 minutes. Add more flour if the sauce refuses to thicken.

Grease a shallow baking dish, then add a layer of tomato sauce, a layer of lasagne, a layer of cheese sauce, a layer of lasagne, and so on, making sure to end up with cheese sauce on top. Then sprinkle on the loose cheese.

Bake in a pre-heated oven for around 25 minutes at Gas Mark 6 (425 Deg F, 220 Deg C).

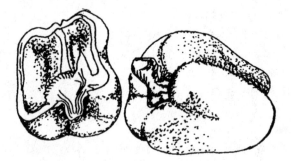

Salads

There are endless recipes for salads, and most people have worked out their own special combinations. Thankfully the days are long gone when a salad consisted only of a limp lettuce leaf, a tiny tomato and a crinkled cucumber. No more could Mr Fawlty respond to a request for a Waldorf Salad with the bluff, "I think we're just out of Waldorfs."

There is an increasing amount of more exotic salad stuff around: some supermarkets stock up to ten different varieties of lettuce alone. But salads are still more popular during the summer months when the produce is cheaper.

Here are some of my favourite recipes.

Pasta salad

Salad with an Italian feel.

Serves 3 to 4

Ingredients

4 oz (100g) of pasta quills or shells
1/2 red pepper, cored and chopped
1/2 green pepper, cored and chopped
A tin of tuna (7 oz)
3 tomatoes, sliced
Black pepper
French dressing, optional

Boil some water in a saucepan and cook the pasta for about 15 minutes or until it is tender, then strain.

Drain the oil from the tuna then mix the ingredients in a serving bowl. Add 2 to 3 tablespoons of dressing if required.

See **Dressing and sauces** section for recipe for French dressing.

Rice and sweetcorn

Ingredients

8 oz (200g) of rice (1 mug)
9 oz (225g) tin of sweetcorn
1 green pepper, cored and chopped into pieces
4 tomatoes, finely chopped
Salt
Pepper
French dressing (see Dressings and sauces)

Wash the rice in a sieve to remove some of the starch. Put the rice in a large saucepan with about a pint of water and a pinch of salt. After the water has boiled, simmer for about 20 to 25 minutes or until the rice is tender, then drain well. Mix all the other ingredients with the rice and pour a little vinaigrette on top.

Salad Niçoise

Ingredients

1 iceberg lettuce
3 tomatoes
1/2 small onion, thinly sliced
2 eggs
8 oz (200g) tin of tuna
Small tin of anchovies, optional
10 olives
French dressing (see Dressings and sauces)

Hard boil the eggs for 8 minutes, then place in a bowl of cold water. Wash the lettuce and arrange the leaves in a large serving bowl, then add the tuna (drain the oil first).

Quarter the tomatoes and place them on top of the lettuce. Shell the eggs, cut them into quarters, and arrange them neatly on top of the tuna. Pour the dressing over the salad, and add the olives, onion and anchovies, if required.

Tomato and onion

A typical Provencal salad. Serves 4.

Ingredients

4 fresh tomatoes
1 onion
Fresh basil
Fresh black pepper
French dressing (see Dressings and sauces)

Peel the onion and slice fairly thinly. Slice the tomatoes and arrange them on a large plate or dish. Place the onion pieces between the tomato slices. Decorate with the basil leaves, and season with plenty of fresh ground pepper. Pour the French dressing over the top.

Potato salad

This recipe can be made with either salad cream or mayonnaise, according to taste. Chopped fresh chives can be added if required. Serves 2.

Ingredients

3 medium sized potatoes
Mayonnaise
Salt
Pepper

If you are using new potatoes the skins can be left on them, otherwise they must be peeled. Place the potatoes in boiling water for 15 minutes or until a knife will pass through the centre fairly easily. After the potatoes have cooled, cut into 1 inch (2.5cm) cubes, place in a bowl and dollop some mayonnaise on top. Mix together and season.

Chopped fresh chives can be added if you like. If you

are using small new potatoes they can be left whole. Another alternative to using mayonnaise is to place new potatoes in bowl with a couple of tablespoons of olive oil.

Avocado and vinaigrette

Avocado is a calorie watcher's nightmare, so if you are trying to slim don't be tempted with this recipe. When choosing an avocado to be eaten straight away make sure it is ripe - it should be slightly soft when the skin is pressed.

Ingredients

1 Avocado
French dressing (see Dressings and sauces)

Remove the skin of the avocado using a knife. Then cut in half, remembering that it is not possible to cut all the way through because there is a avocado stone in the middle (unless you have a chainsaw handy). Cut around the stone, then pull the two halves away from each other. The stone will stay lodged in one side. The easiest way of removing the stone is to stick a sharp knife in it and then ease it out.

After removing the stone, cut the avocado into slices then cover with dressing. Eat immediately.

Coleslaw

Serves 4

Ingredients

1/2 lb (250g) of white cabbage, grated
2 carrots, scraped and grated
1 small onion, peeled and grated
5 to 6 tbs of mayonnaise or salad cream
Salt
Pepper

If you have time, soak the cabbage for an hour to make it crisp. If not, it doesn't really matter. After soaking the cabbage, dry with a kitchen towel and put in a large serving bowl with the carrots and onion. Stir in the mayonnaise, and season.

There are many variations to this recipe. Additional ingredients can include chopped apple, sultanas, and nuts.

Tabouleh

Bulghur wheat is made from wheat that has been boiled, dried, then ground. As an ingredient it is widely used in countries like Morocco and Tunisia.

Serves 4

Ingredients

6 oz (150g) of bulghur wheat
1/8 pint (60ml) of olive oil
1/2 cucumber, chopped
1 tomato, peeled and chopped
1 bunch of spring onions
1 bunch of parsley
8 mint leaves, chopped
Juice of one lemon
Salt
Pepper

Place the bulghur wheat in a saucepan of water. Bring to the boil, then simmer gently for 10 to 15 minutes until tender. Drain, then allow to cool.

Finely chop the parsley and the spring onions. Place the bulghur in a serving bowl, add the olive oil, parsley, mint, tomato, cucumber, spring onions, lemon juice, salt and pepper. Mix together thoroughly.

Snacks and midnight cravings

This is another essential section, since often when breakfast or lunch is skipped a snack can keep the hunger at bay until the evening meal. It is interesting to compare what people regard as a 'snack': for some it is a plate of chips, a pile of sandwiches and a couple of doughnuts, while for others it could be half an apple.

Sandwiches have to be one of the most popular and easy snacks to prepare. I have one friend who I am sure was influenced when he was younger by the children's programme 'Number 73', which featured The Sandwich Game...as well as eating approximately 5000 cheese and salad cream sandwiches in the last 22 years, he eats such combinations as cheese, chocolate and cream. What a sicko!

Stew's cheese sandwiches

A legend in their own right. A snack that can easily be made within the duration of a television commercial break (unless you have to go to the shops to buy some cheese and the shops are miles away and you have to walk there and when you get there the shop is closed for refurbishment).

Serves 1

Ingredients

Bread (brown or white)
Margarine or butter
Cheddar cheese
Salad cream

Butter two or four slices of bread on one side only, slice a single layer of cheese onto one or two of the slices, then spread salad cream onto the other half. Splash the halves together, and cut diagonally for added sophistication. Eat in front of the television or put in a lunch box for a treat later in the day.

Cheese and peanut butter and crisps sandwiches

Serves 1

Ingredients

Bread (brown or white)
Margarine or butter
Cheese (any sort)
Peanut butter
Salt and vinegar crisps

Butter the bread, spread peanut butter onto one half, and put thin slices of cheese onto the other. Cover the cheese with a single layer of crisps, then place the peanut butter-covered slice over the top. Slice into squares, because this sandwich is about as sophisticated as a Lada. Try to eat quietly.

B.L.T.

Otherwise known as a bacon, lettuce and tomato sandwich. Note that this is not your everyday type of sarnie - this is heading towards the realms of haute cuisine, mate!

Serves 1

Ingredients

Butter
3 slices of bread
2 rashers of bacon
A lettuce leaf or two
1 tomato
Salt
Pepper

Remove the crusts from the bread, then slice the tomato. Grill the bacon and the bread. Butter the toast, then place a bit of lettuce, some tomato and a rasher of bacon on it. Put a slice of toast on top and then make up another layer as before. Finish with the last piece of toast on top, then cut diagonally across. Add a dash of salt and pepper if required.

To stop the B.L.T. from falling apart you could try skewering it with a cocktail stick. But under no circumstances should you swallow the cocktail stick in your haste to eat your masterpiece - they are not particularly palatable.

It is a little known fact* that B.L.T.s form the staple diet of a community of ex-gas meter polishers living in a collection of forest huts close to Telford. They claim the sandwich gives them a special 'buzz' and enhances their awareness of dust and other unwanted deposits on gas meters.

* Because it's not actually true.

Bacon and cheese

This for me is the ultimate sandwich...simple, but devastating.

Serves 1

Ingredients

2 slices of bread
2 rashers of bacon
Cheddar cheese
Butter
Tomato sauce

Grill the bacon for a couple of minutes on each side, longer if you prefer it crispy. Whilst the bacon is being grilled, butter the bread and cut a few slices of cheese. When the bacon is cooked place on the bread with the cheese, then squirt some ketchup inside - luvly.

Cheese on toast

A very popular lunchtime snack that can be prepared with tomato on top.

Serves 1

Ingredients

Bread
Cheese

Cover the bread with a thick layer of cheddar cheese, and grill gently until the cheese browns or begins to bubble. Remove from grill, cut in half, and eat immediately before rapid cooling sets in.

Welsh rarebit

Doesn't taste particularly Welsh, nor is it very rare.

Serves 1

Ingredients

6 oz (150g) of cheddar cheese
1/2 oz (15g) of butter or margarine
1/2 tsp of dry mustard
2 tbs of flour
2 slices of bread
4 rashers of streaky bacon

Grate the cheese and put into a small saucepan. Add the butter and mustard, then cook gently, stirring constantly, until the cheese has melted. Take the saucepan away from the heat and add the flour, beating it in until smooth. Allow to cool.

Grill the bacon and the bread, then spread the cheese mixture evenly over the toast. Grill until golden, then add the bacon and serve.

Plain omelette

Serves 1 to 2

Ingredients

2 or 3 eggs
A pinch of mixed herbs
Salt
Pepper
1 oz (25g) of margarine

Beat the eggs together in a mixing bowl and add the

seasoning. Melt the margarine in a frying pan and pour in the eggs. As soon as the eggs start to cook lift up one edge of the omelette with a spatula, tilt the pan and let the uncooked egg run underneath. Continue to do this until the omelette is cooked, then flip it in half and serve on a warmed plate.

Cheese and tomato omelette

Serves 1 to 2

Ingredients

2 or 3 eggs
2 oz (50g) of grated cheese
1 oz (25g) of margarine
1 chopped tomato
Salt
Pepper

Prepare as above, but add the cheese and tomato before adding to the frying pan.

Bacon omelette

Serves 1 to 2

Ingredients

2 or 3 eggs
2 rashers of bacon
Salt
Pepper

Cut the bacon up into little pieces and fry for a couple of minutes, then remove from the pan. Beat the eggs together, season and add the bacon. Melt the margarine in the frying pan and cook using the method described for the plain omelette.

Egg hubble-bubble

Serves 1 to 2

Ingredients

4 potatoes, boiled
Any other vegetables
Butter or margarine
Cheese
4 eggs, lightly beaten and seasoned

Dice the potato, then fry it with any other vegetables you may have (eg mushrooms, tomato, peas) in butter or margarine. When cooked, pour in the eggs and sprinkle with grated cheese. Cook very slowly with a plate or lid over the top, until the eggs are set.

Egg and cheese ramekins

Serves 1

Ingredients

2 oz (50g) of grated cheese
1 egg
1 tomato
Seasoning

Grease a small ovenproof dish, preferably a ramekin dish or one that is about 3 inches (7.5cm) in diameter. Put grated cheese in the bottom of the dish and up the sides. Place in a slice of tomato and then the egg, trying not to break the yolk. Add the seasoning and cover with another slice of tomato and more grated cheese.

Bake in the oven for about 15 minutes at Gas Mark 4 (350 Deg F, 180 Deg C) or until the eggs are set.

Potato and onion fry

Serves 4

Ingredients

1 lb (500g) of potatoes
1 onion
4 rashers of bacon
2 tbs of oil
1 tbs of plain flour
2 eggs, beaten
Pepper

Peel the onion and potatoes, then coarsely grate them and place in a mixing bowl. Add the beaten eggs, bacon and flour, mix together, then season. Heat the oil in a frying pan, then spoon a series of heaped tablespoons of the mixture into the pan. Fry the potato cakes on both sides till they turn a golden brown. Continue doing this until all the mixture is used up.

Serve with a baked beans or a salad.

Puds, biccies and cakes

Victoria sponge

Ingredients

4 oz (100g) of self-raising flour
4 oz (100g) of margarine
4 oz (100g) of caster sugar
2 eggs, beaten
Jam

(Two 7 inch / 17cm sandwich tins are needed)

Mix together the sugar and margarine until they are smooth in texture. Gradually add the eggs to the mixture, then fold in the flour. Divide the mixture between the two baking tins (these need to be greased first, which means wiping the inside with a piece of greaseproof paper covered with fat - never spray with WD40). Make sure that the tops of the cakes are level, then bake in the oven for 20 minutes or so at Gas Mark 5 (400 Deg F, 200 Deg C).

The way to see if a cake is cooked is to stick a skewer or a knitting needle in the centre of the sponge. If bits of the mixture are stuck to it when it is drawn out, it needs to be cooked a little longer. If the skewer comes out clean, the cake is ready.

Now turn the cakes out of the tins onto a wire rack (look in the grill pan for one). Once cooled, spread a layer of jam over one of the layers, sandwich the other one on top, and sprinkle with caster sugar.

Rock buns

Ingredients

8 oz (200g) of self-raising flour
4 oz (100g) of margarine
3 oz (75g) of currants or raisins
A pinch of nutmeg
3 oz (75g) of sugar
1 egg, beaten
2 tbs of milk
A pinch of salt

Mix the flour, nutmeg and salt together. Then rub the flour and margarine together until they look like breadcrumbs. The next stage is to add the currants, sugar, egg and milk. The mixture should be fairly firm.

Grease a baking tray with some margarine. Mould the mixture into small lumps and place on the baking tray. Bake for 20 minutes, Gas Mark 6 (425 Deg F, 220 Deg C).

Iced choccy cake

Ingredients

6 oz (150g) of self-raising flour
6 oz (150g) of margarine
6 oz (150g) of caster sugar
3 eggs
1 1/2 oz (40g) of cocoa
1 1/2 tbs of water

(For the icing)
8 oz (200g) of icing sugar
4 oz (100g) of plain cooking chocolate
1 1/2 oz (40g) of butter/margarine
2 tbs of warm water

Place the sugar and the margarine in a large mixing bowl and mix together, using either a wooden spoon or an electric mixer (which will save time). Add the eggs, one at a time.

In a separate bowl, mix the flour and the cocoa powder together, then add it to the creamed mixture. Continue mixing, adding water until a soft dropping consistency is achieved. Divide the mixture equally between two 7 inch (17cm) sandwich tins. Bake in the oven at Gas Mark 5 (400 Deg F, 200 Deg C) for 25 to 30 minutes.

Test the cake with a skewer. If the mixture sticks to it, the cake needs a few more minutes in the oven.

When the cakes are ready, turn them out of their tins onto a wire rack (if available). Melt the chocolate by placing it in a basin and putting that over the top of a saucepan of boiling water. Be careful not to let the water boil over the top of the saucepan into the chocolate.

After the chocolate has melted, allow to cool. Cream together the butter and half the icing sugar, then add half the melted chocolate. Mix, and spread over one side of the cake, then 'sandwich' the two together.

The rest of the chocolate is used to make the icing on the top. Add the water and sugar to the chocolate, and spoon onto the top of the cake. Spread the icing around using a palette knife that has been dipped in hot water (this helps to spread the icing and stop it sticking to the knife). The cake can be decorated with those little silver balls that break your teeth, or with tasteful designs of snooker tables etc.

Baked apples

Ingredients

1 large cooking apple per person
Mincemeat
Brown sugar
Butter

Remove the cores from the apples and stand them in an ovenproof dish. Fill the hole in the apple with mincemeat and a teaspoon of brown sugar. Add a nob of butter on top.

Put enough water in the dish to cover the bottom of the apples. Bake at Gas Mark 4 (350 Deg F, 180 Deg C) for about an hour. After an hour test the apple with a skewer. It should be soft, but not too much. Serve with cream.

Grandma's chocolate chip cookies

This is one of my Grandmother's recipes. I would like to thank her for the regular supply of these cookies and all the other things she makes for me.

Ingredients

6 oz (150g) of self-raising flour
3 oz (75g) of margarine
3 oz (75g) of granulated sugar
1 oz (25g) of brown sugar
2 drops of vanilla essence
4 oz (100g) of chopped cooking chocolate
1 egg

Cream the margarine and the sugars either in a mixer or with a wooden spoon. Beat in the egg and vanilla. Grate or chop the chocolate coarsely, then stir into the creamed mixture with the flour. Using a teaspoon make into balls and place on a greased flat baking tin. Bake in the centre of the oven for about 15 minutes at Gas Mark 5 (400 Deg F, 200 Deg C). Place on a wire tray and leave until cold.

Raspberry buns

Ingredients

8 oz (200g) of self-raising flour
4 oz (100g) of caster sugar
3 oz (75g) of margarine
1 egg, beaten
1 tbs of milk
A pinch of salt

Rub the margarine and flour together using your fingertips, until the mixture resembles breadcrumbs. Add the sugar, egg, and milk, and mix well. The mixture should be quite stiff.

Grease a baking tray, then shape the mixture into twelve balls and place on the tray. Make a little hole on the top and fill with a teaspoon of jam.

Bake in the oven on Gas Mark 7 (425 Deg F, 220 Deg C) for about 20 minutes.

Flapjacks

For those with access to two baking trays and living in a large household it can be advisable to double the quantities given here, as flapjacks tend to be incredibly popular. Alternatively, the recipe can be made a little less popular by changing the ingredients - try adding peanut butter, or raisins and nuts.

Ingredients

8 oz (200g) of porridge oats
4 oz (100g) of margarine
3 oz (75g) of sugar
4 level tbs of golden syrup
A pinch of salt

Melt the margarine in a large saucepan, then add the syrup and leave over a low heat for a couple of minutes. Remove from the heat and add the sugar, salt and oats. Mix thoroughly using a wooden spoon, making sure all the oats are covered with syrup.

Grease a shallow baking tray and evenly spoon in the mixture. Cook for 20 to 30 minutes at Gas Mark 4 (350 Deg F, 180 Deg C). After cooking, cut the flapjacks into bars before they cool.

Scones

Ingredients

**8 oz (200g) of plain flour
2 oz (50g) of margarine
1/4 pint (125ml) of milk
A pinch of salt**

Mix the flour and salt together. The flour is supposed to be sieved, but it's a bit time-consuming and doesn't make much difference anyway. Cut the margarine into small cubes and add them to the flour. Rub the mixture using your fingers, continuing until the result looks like breadcrumbs.

Add the milk and stir in using the blade of a knife to form a soft dough. Roll out the mixture on a floured board until it is about 1/2 an inch (1.5cm) thick. Cut into rounds using a biscuit cutter or a glass.

Grease a baking tray and place some scones on it, leaving enough gaps for them to rise. Brush some milk over the top of the scones to obtain a smooth and shiny finish.

Bake in the oven for 10 to 15 minutes at Gas Mark 7 (450 Deg F, 230 Deg C).

Cheese scones

As for above, but stir in 4 oz (100g) of cheese before adding the milk.

Fruit scones

As for plain scones, but stir in 1 oz (25g) of sugar and 2 oz (50g) of dried fruit, sultanas, currants etc.

Toasted marshmallows

Ingredients

1 packet of pink or white marshmallows

Lay the marshmallows on a piece of foil (to prevent them from falling through the grid into the grill pan) and place them under a medium grill. Turn them so that they cook evenly. They will puff up and turn golden brown. Eat immediately.

Baked bananas

Ingredients

1 banana
Brown or golden granulated sugar
Lemon juice

Pre-heat the oven to Gas Mark 4 (350 Deg F, 180 Deg C). Peel the banana and place it on a piece of foil, shiny side uppermost, making sure the foil is large enough to wrap it up loosely. Squeeze the lemon juice over the banana, sprinkle with brown sugar, and loosely wrap up.

Place in the centre of the oven on a baking tray and bake until it is slightly soft to touch.

Serve with cream or ice cream.

Lemon snow

Serves 4 to 6

Ingredients

2 lemons
3 tbs of sugar
2 tsp of gelatine
2 egg whites

Grate the lemon rind and squeeze the juice from the lemons. Place the juice and the rind in a small bowl, add the sugar, and sprinkle gelatine on top. Leave until it becomes spongy.

Place the bowl in a saucepan of hot water and heat until the gelatine has dissolved, stirring occasionally. Make sure the water doesn't boil over into the juice. Leave to cool.

Beat the egg whites until stiff, then fold in the gelatine mixture and pile into small dishes or one large bowl.

Decorate with grated chocolate.

Raspberry brulée

Serves 4

Ingredients

**1/2 lb (250g) of fresh raspberries
1/2 pint (0.25 litre) of double cream
6 oz (150g) of Demerara sugar or golden granulated**

Place the raspberries in a shallow heatproof dish. Whip the cream until thick, (but not too stiff) and spread over the raspberries. Sprinkle sugar over the cream, covering it completely.

Pre-heat the grill and then place the brulée under the grill, until it is dark and bubbling.

Remove from the grill and cool. Chill in the fridge for a couple of hours.

A cheaper version could be made using sliced banana.

Poached peaches

Serves 4

Ingredients

**Tin of peach halves
1/2 oz (15g) of butter or margarine**

2 tbs of brown or golden granulated sugar
1 tbs of brandy or whisky, optional

Drain the syrup from the peaches, reserving a small amount.
Melt the butter in a saucepan. Add the peaches with the
syrup and sugar.

Heat gently for about 5 minutes then stir in any
flavouring. If you have any flaked almonds or nuts, a few of
these toasted and sprinkled on top will add great excitement
to your life.

Orange chiffon pie

Serves 4 to 6

Ingredients

6 oz (150g) of digestive biscuits
2 oz (50g) of sugar, Demerara or granulated
3 oz (75g) of butter or margarine

Crush the biscuits by putting a few at a time between 2
sheets of greaseproof paper or in a paper bag and then
attacking them with a rolling pin or a milk bottle (milk
cartons are no good for this). Transfer each load of crumbs
to a bowl until all the biscuits are done.

Melt the butter in a saucepan, then add the biscuit
crumbs and sugar, and mix them together. Press the
mixture into a flan or sandwich tin and chill in the
refrigerator for half an hour.

For the filling -

2 oranges
4 tbs of orange squash, undiluted
2 oz (50g) of caster sugar
2 eggs
2 tbs of cornflour

Grate the orange rind and save it. Squeeze the juice and put it into a measuring jug. Add the orange squash and make up to 1/2 pint (0.25 litre) with water. Mix the cornflour and sugar together in a small bowl and add a small amount of juice. Stir until the mixture becomes a smooth paste.

Separate the eggs, then place the cornflour in a thick bottomed saucepan and stir in the egg yolks using a wooden spoon. Add the remainder of the juice and the grated orange rinds, and when thoroughly mixed place on a low heat. Stir continuously until the mixture thickens.

Remove the pan from the heat and leave to cool, stirring frequently to avoid lumpiness.

Warm up the oven, and while it is doing so whisk the egg whites until stiff, then using a spoon fold this into the orange mixture, making sure it is smooth and evenly mixed. Place the filling onto the biscuit base, then bake in the centre of the oven on gas mark 6 (430 Deg F, 225 Deg C) for about 15 minutes.

When it has cooked place it in the fridge to cool.

Batters

Yorkshire pudding

Ingredients

4 oz (100g) of plain flour
1 egg, beaten
1/2 pint (0.25 litre) of milk, or milk and water
Oil
A pinch of salt

Mix the salt and flour together in a mixing bowl, then make a 'well' in the flour and add the egg. Mix in the flour carefully, adding a little milk until all the flour is mixed in, then add the remaining milk. Beat the mixture for a few minutes until it is smooth. Pour a teaspoon of oil into the individual patty tins, then add 2 tablespoons of the mixture into each. Bake for about 15 minutes or until they have risen and browned.

Pancakes

Serves 4

Ingredients

4 oz (100g) of plain flour
1 egg
1/2 pint (0.25 litre) of milk
A pinch of salt
Butter
Sugar (or any other topping)

Put the flour and salt in a bowl and add the egg into the middle. Pour in about a third of the milk. Stir gently, adding a little more milk in the process. Beat the mixture thoroughly, then add the rest of the milk. Stir well, then pour into a jug.

Melt a small piece of butter in a frying pan, then add a couple of tablespoons of the batter. Tip the frying pan to spread the mixture evenly. Fry until the underside is brown, then toss the pancake.

Scrape the mess resulting from the dropped pancake off the floor, then start again. This time, when the underside is brown, turn it over with a fish slice or a knife and cook the other side.

Tip the finished pancake onto a plate and cover with lemon juice and sugar.

Pineapple in batter

This is a nice and easy pud, and can also be made using a banana - just slice the banana lengthways and dip it in the batter, then fry until golden. Serves 4.

Ingredients

4 oz (100g) of plain flour
1 egg
1/4 pint (125ml) of milk
A tin of pineapple rings
2 tbs of oil

Prepare the mixture as with the pancakes, then dip a pineapple ring in the batter and fry until the batter turns a golden brown.

Breakfast time

Supposedly the most important meal of the day, but all too often rushed or ignored altogether.

Cereal

Huge variety here, from the standard Cornflakes to the more exotic muesli. From a health point of view the cereals aimed at children (with added chocolate, frosted sugar etc) should be avoided, in favour of those with a higher bran content and with no added sugar.

Cereals are the easiest meals to prepare, and most cereal breakfasts will contain nearly all the nutrients needed each day. In fact, if you are stuck for food at any other time of day, you could do a lot worse than pour out another bowl of them.

Milk is one of nature's healthiest products, and half a pint poured onto breakfast cereals every morning is a sure way of ensuring a regular intake. But full cream milk can be fattening, so try to use semi skimmed, which is fast becoming the norm in many households. Keen dieters who want to use skimmed milk will find they quickly get used to it.

If you normally pour spoonfuls of sugar onto cereal, try cutting down a little each day, and make up for the loss of flavour by adding some fresh fruit like apple, banana, strawberries or raspberries. If you don't have any fresh fruit add a handful of raisins.

Eggs

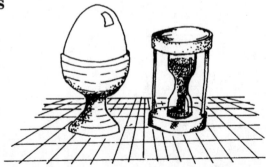

Health risk

There is a health risk. Probably. Ask Edwina for more advice.

Scrambled Egg

Serves 2

Ingredients

3 eggs
1 oz (25g) of butter
4 tbs of milk
Pepper

Whisk the eggs in a bowl and add the milk and pepper. Melt the butter in a saucepan and add the egg mixture. Stir the mixture as it thickens. Don't have the heat up too high, or else the egg will burn and stick to the pan.

Serve on top of hot buttered toast.

Poached egg

Ingredients

1 egg per person!
Butter or margarine

Put a nob of butter in one of the poacher rings, add the egg and cook for about 4 minutes, according to taste.

Boiled egg

Ingredients

1 egg

Boil some water in a saucepan and carefully lower the egg into the water, using a spoon. Then boil for 3 to 4 minutes, depending on how runny you want the egg to be.

After removing the egg from the water, whack the top with a spoon - this will stop the egg from hardening.

If you require the egg to be hard boiled, cook for about 8 minutes in boiling water.

If your egg cracks whilst it is cooking pour a tablespoon of vinegar in the water - this will seal the crack.

Fried egg

Ingredients

1 egg
2 tbs of oil

Pour some oil in a frying pan, but don't let the fat get too hot, otherwise the egg will stick to the pan and bubble. Crack the egg on the side of the pan and plop the egg into the oil. Fry gently for about 3 minutes, basting occasionally. If you like your eggs American style (sunny side down), fry both sides of the egg.

Eggy bread

Ingredients

3 eggs
4 tbs of milk
Slices of bread without the crusts
2 tbs of oil
Pepper

Beat the eggs and the milk together and season. Heat the oil in a frying pan. Dip a slice of bread in the egg mixture and then fry for a couple of minutes on each side.

Dippy-in soldiers

Ingredients

1 soft boiled egg
Bread and butter

For those who want to relive the delights of childhood, cut the crusts off the bread, butter it and then cut into 1 inch (2.5cm) wide strips. Then take your soldier and dip it in the yolk part of the egg. I think only the British could come up with something as odd as this.

Egg surprise

Ingredients

Anything with no egg in it.

Guide to entertaining

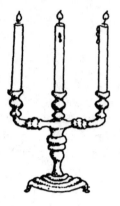

Preparation

During your time at college there are probably going to be times when you might decide that instead of going down the pub or to a nightclub it would make a nice change to have a few friends round to dinner. It won't necessarily be a grand affair and doesn't have to cost a great deal of money: if everybody chips in a couple of quid it will normally cover the cost of the food. There will also be times when perhaps you want to cook a romantic meal for two, and with restaurant prices being on the somewhat expensive side it will save you quite a bit of dosh.

There are no set guidelines on what you should serve. It will often depend on how much money, time and effort you want to put into it. There are many recipes that can be used from previous sections that are simple and inexpensive, and ideal for informal supper parties, but a few more are included in this section..

One of the nicest things about having people round to dinner is that it gives you a chance to have a good pig out for a lot less than the price of several restaurant meals. If you would normally go out to the pub where it is impossible to have a conversation over the noise of the jukebox, a dinner party can be a wonderful chance to discuss the future of the planet, the political state of the country, and the price of beer in the union bar.

Example recipes -

Chicken Al style

Serves 4

Ingredients

2 tbs of oil
3 chicken breasts
Juice of 2 lemons
1 tbs of sherry
1 tsp of French mustard
Fresh black pepper

This dish needs to be prepared a little in advance. If you don't have any sherry, wine could be used, or it could be omitted.

Remove the skin from the chicken if it has not already been done. Dice the chicken breasts into bite sized pieces and put in a small mixing bowl along with the lemon juice, mustard, sherry and pepper. Mix well and leave for 1/2 hour or more.

After your chicken has been sitting in the marinade for 1/2 an hour or so it's ready for cooking. Heat the oil in a frying pan, then gently fry the chicken for about 10 minutes.

The chicken can be served with fresh vegetables of your choice. See vegetables section for advice on preparing veg. If it is a special occasion why not try something different like mangetout.

Pasta with salmon and mushrooms

This recipe takes about 15 minutes to make but tastes as though you have spent all afternoon preparing it! Very handy if you have to impress guests at short notice.

Serves 2

Ingredients

4 oz (100g) of Tagliatelli
1 tin of condensed mushroom soup
2 oz (50g) of mushrooms, sliced
1 tin of salmon
Salt

Put the Tagliatelli in a saucepan of boiling water with a pinch salt. Pour the soup into a saucepan, then add the mushrooms and salmon. Stir until hot, being careful not to allow it to boil. A little milk may be added if the sauce is too thick. When the pasta is cooked, this should take about 15 minutes, drain and pour the sauce over it. Garnish with parsley.

Mike's Caribbean Kebabs

Serves 4

Ingredients

11/2 lb (750g) of diced pork
10 rashers of streaky bacon
2 red peppers
3 bananas
1 large tin of pineapple rings

For the marinade:

4 tbs of golden syrup
6 tbs of soy sauce
6 tbs of pineapple juice
1 tbs of tomato puree
1 oz (25g) of fresh ginger
Black pepper

Mix all the ingredients of the marinade together in a bowl, then place the pork in it and leave in the fridge for 6 hours or more.

Seed the peppers and cut into 1 inch (2.5cm) pieces. Cut the bananas crossways into 1 inch (2.5cm) lengths and wrap each piece of banana in half a rasher of bacon. Cut the pineapple rings into 1 inch (2.5cm) sections.

Thread the above onto the skewers starting and ending with the red pepper. Thread the banana crossways to hold the bacon in place.

Baste with marinade then put in the oven at Gas Mark 7 (450 Deg F, 230 Deg C) for 20 to 30 minutes, basting regularly with any spare marinade. Serve with rice.

Steaks

The most popular steaks are rump, fillet, sirloin and entrecote. Fillet is the most tender and lean, but unfortunately the most expensive.

Steaks are best grilled or fried:

To grill

Brush the steaks with butter and season with black pepper. Make sure the grill is hot before you cook the steaks. Grill each side for 3 to 4 minutes, if you want the steaks dripping with blood cook for slightly less time or eat raw. If you like your steaks well done cook for about 5 to 6 minutes on each side.

To fry

Heat a nob of butter in a frying pan then put in the steak. Fry quickly for a couple of minutes to seal in the flavour. Turn down the heat, cook for 5 minutes for 'rare', 5 to 7 minutes for medium and 15 minutes for charcoal.

The above times for both grilling and frying will depend on the thickness of the steak.

Serve the steaks with fried potatoes, or new potatoes and fresh vegetables.

Accessories - napkins etc

These all increase the cost of the dinner party, but they will usually be expected by the guests. Try to buy cheap napkins, since they'll only be thrown away later. Candles should not cost the earth, and they can be stuck stylishly in the necks of empty wine bottles.

Cutlery

Getting enough cutlery can be a challenge, and asking guests to bring their own is not really the done thing. The only thing for it is to actually do the washing up (it needed doing anyway, let's face it) and then count the forks etc. If matching sets are available then so much the better.

Booze

This is one subject that most students seem to have a natural ability to understand, and a great deal of time is given by students to gaining the most from this area of knowledge. Some of the recipes in this book contain wine, but often it is optional (they just taste better if you can afford it).

Wine

The standard offering at a dinner party tends to be wine. Normally guests will bring a bottle of wine with them but buy a few bottles in case they don't.

The availability and consumption of wine in Britain is probably the highest it has ever been, which goes some way to explaining why it is no longer regarded as a snobbish drink. The price of wine in Britain is painfully expensive compared to prices among our European neighbours, though this is not a totally bad thing since it justifies day-trips to France. In Britain it is rare to find a bottle for under £2, and if you do it will probably be fit only for cooking.

My knowledge of wine is purely based on experimentation, which is probably the most enjoyable way to gain familiarity. Those who are already connoisseurs will probably find this section irrelevant.

Apart from the obvious wine growing countries like

France, Germany, Spain and Portugal there are several countries that have made huge investments in vineyards, and have since become serious contenders in the wine market. The heavy investment especially in America has made use of new technology that has left the methods used by the French and other European countries looking somewhat dated.

The Australians have also come up with some excellent wines recently, many of which are very reasonably priced. Don't be put off by names like 'Seaview' - I know it sounds more like a British seaside guesthouse, but the taste is the important thing. Some other excellent value wines come from Bulgaria, like the Bulgarian Country Wines.

Choose whatever wine you prefer. It doesn't really matter whether you serve red wine with fish or white wine with red meat. I personally rarely drink white wine because I prefer red or rose.

German white wine tends to be sweeter than the French whites, and this has helped Leibfraumilch to became a household name during the 1980's.

Red wine should normally be served at room temperature, exceptions being if the room is an igloo or steel smelting plant.

White should be chilled before serving.

Mulled wine

Good after bonfire night or at Christmas.

Ingredients

1 bottle of red wine
4 to 6 tsp of sugar
The rind of 1 orange or lemon
2 inch stick of cinnamon
A blade of mace
2 cloves
Slices of orange/lemon for serving

Heat the wine and sugar, but do not allow to boil. Then add the orange and spices. Strain and serve.

Booze-ups

Few students need to learn anything more about this familiar subject. A booze-up may be pre-arranged, or may follow quite naturally from the dinner party. A common scenario is for the wine/lager to run out soon after the meal, resulting in a mad rush to get to the off-licence before it shuts. This can be avoided with a little forward planning - pool the house money (or dip into the week's kitty) and buy cheap alcohol from a large supermarket. This should save a bit of money and panic in the long run.

Before a booze-up takes place it is important to remove all objects that might suffer its effects: neighbours, landlords, televisions, the entire house. In fact, it is far better to hold it in someone else's house or on a beach etc. A surprising number of videos, CD players, and half-written essays suffer untimely demises in the hands of spilt beer at these events, so take care.

Punches

These things are produced in bulk, and are not intended for the lone drinker. The quantities involved are such that a plastic beer-brewing barrel is probably the best thing to mix it in. Or the bath. Coloured effects can be obtained by using orange juice or Ribena.

Punches are another way to save money at a booze-up. Strong drinks will go further when they are mixed with orange juice or lemonade or whatever. But some punches can be deadly, so check exactly what is going into the mixture, preferably sticking to a pre-agreed plan or recipe. The completed punch can then be poured back into its component bottles, so that everyone should have a litre or so to themselves.

Here's a couple of easy punches to get things swinging...

Rum punch

Ingredients

1 pint (0.5 litre) of white rum
5 pints (2.5 litres) of orange juice
1 pint (0.5 litre) of grapefruit juice
Dash of grenadine
1 orange, sliced

Mix the above ingredients together and serve with paper umbrellas if required!

Fizzy fruit punch

Ingredients

2 bottles of sparkling wine
3 measures of brandy
2 miniature bottles of maraschino liqueur
2 peaches
8 oz (200g) of fresh strawberries
3 tbs of sugar

Remove the stones from the peaches, then cut them into pieces. Cut the strawberries into slices and put then with the peaches in a large bowl. Add the sugar, brandy and the maraschino and leave for a while. Just before serving add the chilled wine and serve immediately.

Money saving tips

If times are hard, and most people who have been a student will have at some point experienced the situation in which the bank refuses to give you any more money and then eats your cash card, every penny you can get hold of will have to be wisely spent.

Food is something that we cannot live without, in spite of what some dieters seem to think, so money has to be found from somewhere to keep us alive. But when this seems impossible, the first rule of survival is to check in the cupboard, and freezer if you have one, to see what food is already there. Try to use up whatever is still safely edible, even if it means making up your own concoctions.

When buying food, cut out all non essential items like crisps, chocolate, biscuits and ready to cook meals. These things are expensive, and those on the poverty line will find that cutting down on these items for a couple of weeks can save a significant amount of money. There is no point in buying ready made meals - they may save time, but then how much is your time worth? Very little, probably. These meals are extortionately expensive and their equivalents can be prepared for a fraction of the price at home.

Economising

Cooking for one is relatively more expensive that cooking for 2 or more. Economists will recognise that this is connected with economies of scale, or something like that.

When shopping, look out for special offers or reduced items. Designing a menu around these bargains can be an interesting challenge as well as a money saver. If you can foresee the approach of long period of poverty then buy food in bulk. Although it means spending a large amount in one go, it should in the long run save money. Items like rice and pasta are cheaper pound for pound if you buy in bulk.

It is important to remember when economising on food that the essential nutrients and the other things described in the chapter on healthy eating must remain part of your diet. It might be worthwhile investing in a bottle or a packet of multi vitamins, to be on the safe side.

Conclusion

Well, it's the end of the book. Presumably you've bothered to read the rest of it before wondering what this page is all about? No? Well go and read it, because I want to talk only to those who have been on a culinary journey with me, a journey that has taken us through many fine countries of the world, and a journey on which only the finest food was eaten...

You are now a well travelled, gastronomically speaking, student cook, and are probably full from trying so many wonderful recipes. The only thing now to do is to remember that these recipes should remain part of your diet after you leave college and are forced to discover the real world. Life will get tough, pressures will increase, the daily dose of stress will become as common as the daily sessions of 'Neighbours', but deep down you will know that when you get home you will be able to cook a fine meal. Alternatively, why not escape from the real world altogether and make up a barrel of punch?

Whatever happens, I hope this book has been as entertaining as it has been useful, and that after reading it your housemates will be astounded by your newly acquired culinary skill and imagination. Well, let's just hope you don't make them sick, anyway.

Bon appetit!

Index

FOUNDED 1965

OVER 80 RESTAURANTS THROUGHOUT THE COUNTRY

The Student Standby

Head Office: Kensal Road, London, W10 5BN Telephone 0181-960 8238

PIZZA EXPRESS RESTAURANTS IN GREAT BRITAIN

Location	Phone	Location	Phone
WARDOUR STREET, SOHO, W1	0171-734 0355	ST ANDREWS STREET, CAMBRIDGE	01223 61320
DEAN STREET, SOHO, W1	0171-437 9595	JESUS LANE, CAMBRIDGE	01223 324033
BARRETT ST, ST CHRISTOPHER'S PLACE, W1	0171-629 1001	BEST LANE, CANTERBURY, KENT	01227 766938
THE COLONNADES, BAYSWATER, W2	0171-229 7784	MOULSHAM STREET, CHELMSFORD, ESSEX	01245 491466
CHISWICK HIGH ROAD, W4	0181-747 0193	BELGRAVE HO, IMPERIAL SQ, CHELTENHAM	01242 253896
BOND STREET, EALING, W5	0181-567 7690	SOUTH STREET, CHICHESTER, WEST SUSSEX	01243 786648
EARLS COURT ROAD, KENSINGTON, W8	0171-937 0761	ST RUNWALD STREET, COLCHESTER, ESSEX	01206 760680
NOTTING HILL GATE, W11	0171-229 6000	SOUTH END, CROYDON	0181-680 0123
ROCKLEY ROAD, SHEPHERDS BUSH, W14	0181-749 8582	HIGH STREET, DORKING, SURREY	01306 888236
COPTIC STREET, BLOOMSBURY, WC1	0171-636 3232	SOUTH STREET, EPSOM, SURREY	01372 729618
BOW STREET, COVENT GARDEN, WC2	0171-240 3443	QUEEN STREET, GLASGOW	0141-221 3333
MONTAGUE CLOSE, SOUTHWARK, SE1	0171-378 6446	HIGH STREET, GUILDFORD	01483 300 122
TRANQUIL VALE, BLACKHEATH, SE3	0181-318 2595	COLLEGE ROAD, HARROW, MIDDLESEX	0181-427 9195
WESTOW HILL, CRYSTAL PALACE, SE19	0181-670 1786	OXFORD STREET, HIGH WYCOMBE	01494 558100
VICTORIA STREET, SW1	0171-828 1477	HIGH STREET, KINGSTON UPON THAMES	0181-546 1447
FULHAM ROAD, FULHAM, SW6	0171-731 3117	THE WHITE CLOTH HALL, CROWN ST, LEEDS	0113 246 5207
GLOUCESTER ROAD, SW7	0171-584 9078	KING STREET, LEICESTER	0116 254 4144
FULHAM ROAD, CHELSEA, SW10	0171-352 5300	VICTORIA STREET, LIVERPOOL	0151-236 4987
BATTERSEA BRIDGE ROAD, SW11	0171-924 2774	HIGH ROAD, LOUGHTON, ESSEX	0181-508 3303
LAVENDER HILL, BATTERSEA, SW11	0171-223 5677	EARL STREET, MAIDSTONE, KENT	01622 683549
UPPER RICHMOND RD WEST, E. SHEEN, SW14	0181-878 6833	SOUTH KING ST, MANCHESTER	0161-834 0145
UPPER RICHMOND ROAD, PUTNEY, SW15	0181-789 1948	MIDSUMMER BOULEVARD, MILTON KEYNES	01908 231738
OLD YORK RD, WANDSWORTH TOWN, SW18	0181-877 9812	BENEDICT STREET, NORWICH	01603 622157
HIGH STREET, WIMBLEDON, SW19	0181-946 6027	KING STREET, NOTTINGHAM	0115 952 9095
UPPER STREET, ISLINGTON, N1	0171-226 9542	THE GOLDEN CROSS, OXFORD	01865 790442
MUSWELL HILL BROADWAY, N10	0181-883 5845	ST MARY'S BUTTS, READING, BERKSHIRE	01734 391920
HIGH ROAD, NORTH FINCHLEY, N12	0181-445 7714	HILL STREET, RICHMOND, SURREY	0181-940 8951
FINCHLEY ROAD, SWISS COTTAGE, NW3	0171-794 5100	HIGH STREET, RUISLIP, MIDDLESEX	01895 625100
GOLDERS GREEN RD, GOLDERS GREEN, NW11	0181-455 9556	BLUE BOAR ROW, SALISBURY	01722 415191
38 DAWSON STREET, DUBLIN		OXFORD STREET, SOUTHAMPTON	01703 499090
HIGH STREET, BARNET, HERTS	0181-449 3706	LONDON ROAD, SOUTHEND, ESSEX	01702 435585
WHITE HO, WINCHESTER RD, BASINGSTOKE	01256 54439	VERULAM ROAD, ST ALBANS, HERTS	01727 853020
BARTON STREET, BATH, AVON	01225 420119	HALKETT PLACE, ST. HELIER, JERSEY	01534 33291
HIGH STREET, BECKENHAM, KENT	0181-650 0593	CLARENCE STREET, STAINES, MIDDLESEX	01784 456522
HIGH STREET, BERKHAMPSTEAD	01442 879966	HIGH STREET, SUTTON, SURREY	0181-643 4725
CITADEL, CORPORATION ST, BIRMINGHAM	0121-236 0221	YORK STREET, TWICKENHAM, MIDDLESEX	0181-891 4126
BRINDLEY PLACE, BROAD ST, BIRMINGHAM	0121 643 2500	HIGH STREET, WATFORD	01923 213991
HIGH STREET, BRENTWOOD, ESSEX*	01277 233569	HIGH ROAD, WEMBLEY, MIDDLESEX	0181-902 4918
PRINCE ALBERT ST, THE LANES, BRIGHTON	01273 323205	BRIDGE STREET, WINCHESTER, HAMPSHIRE	01962 841845
BERKELEY SQUARE, BRISTOL, AVON*	0117 926 0300	GOLDSWORTH ROAD, WOKING	01483 750310
WIDMORE ROAD, BROMLEY	0181-464 2708	STANFORD SQ, WARWICK ST, WORTHING	01903 821133
PARK STREET, CAMBERLEY, SURREY*	01276 21846	RIVER HOUSE, MUSEUM STREET, YORK	01904 672904

Licensing hours at Pizza Express are generally: Weekdays 11.30 am - Midnight, Sunday Midday - 11.30 pm
*Local licensing hours may differ at certain restaurants. The law permits 1/2-hour "drinking up" time.

Other books from Summersdale

VOLUNTARY WORK ABROAD

Corinna Thomas

Foreword by
Mark Tully
BBC India Correspondent

New edition

£5.99 (paperback)

The Busker's Guide To Europe

How to make a fortune from your talents (and get a free holiday!)

Stewart Ferris
£5.95 (paperback)

DON'T LEAN OUT OF THE WINDOW!
Surviving Europe on a Train

The Inter Rail travelogue

"It's nothing but bad language, bad taste, absent morals, and a damning indictment of modern youth. I loved it!"

Stewart Ferris & Paul Bassett
£4.95 (paperback)

How To Chat-up Women

Matt Mountebank
£6.99 (paperback)

Classic Love Poems

£10.99 (hardback)

How To Become A Millionaire

Advice and business plans for the serious entrepreneur

CHARLES RYDER
£6.99 (paperback)

How To Save Money

RICHARD BENSON
£5.99 (paperback)

Household Hints

EMMA ANDREWS
£5.99 (paperback)

REAL SELF DEFENCE

GEOFF THOMPSON
£12.99 (paperback)

These books are available through all good bookshops. In case of difficulty, write to us enclosing a cheque or postal order payable to SUMMERSDALE PUBLISHERS. Please add £1 p&p per book if ordering from within UK, £3 p&p per book if ordering from overseas.
Send to: Summersdale Publishers, PO Box 49, Chichester, PO19 2FJ, England